CAREER DIRECTIONING

CAREER DIRECTIONING

A Practical Guide for Job Seekers

GLENN A. DRUHOT

Library of Congress Control Number:		2007903074
ISBN:	Hardcover	978-1-4257-6643-6
	Softcover	978-1-4257-6631-3

This book was printed in the United States of America.

Cover design and layout: Janelle Young

Author Photo: Janelle Young

To order additional copies of this book, contact:
Xlibris Corporation
1-888-795-4274
www.Xlibris.com
Orders@Xlibris.com
38928

CONTENTS

DEDICATION

I am grateful for the thousands of former clients, students, associates and friends that I have met through my career coaching practice. I have considered it a privilege helping them find careers that are satisfying. This book is also dedicated to my wife who has been there cheering me on and the countless others who have championed the idea of finally getting this book published.

George Elliot stated it eloquently when he said *"It is never too late to become who you might have been."* That is the dream that I hold in my heart for everyone who reads this book.

What is Career Directioning?

CAREER DIRECTIONING IS a process of discovering what career you would be best suited for and enjoy the most. This book is intended to help you find your *perfect* career. My goal is to assist you in finding the right position—not just another job. Career Directioning entails our strengths that motivate us with the challenge, recognition or opportunity for growth we are seeking. This book is designed in a workbook format to assist you in your career management. The chapters are deliberately sequenced in a logical order so that each chapter builds upon the previous one. Throughout the book are stories of clients with whom I have worked over the years. Some of those I have coached listened and then acted upon their revelations and have certainly changed the direction of their lives. These stories help to illustrate the required steps to a successful job search campaign.

> *"To be what you are and to become what you are capable of becoming is the only purpose of life."* —Robert Lewis Stevenson

There is a myth of job security in our country. What is job security anyway? I have two magnets sitting on my desk at the office, which symbolically represent the misconception of job security. One is clearly labeled JOB and the other is labeled SECURITY. If you try to place them together they repel each other. Job security no longer lies with a large corporation or organization. Job security lies within the individual and how he or she feels about their own skills and abilities. The more secure you are with what you have to offer an employer in the way of real skills and abilities, the more marketable you are to them. The days of working for the same employer for 20, 30 or more years is all but gone. Now days, people tend to out grow their jobs. When no longer satisfied with nor excited about a position, they look for a different company to employ them. Then, of course, there is constant worry of a job loss due to downsizing, right sizing, reengineering, or flattening of the organization. Over the past 20 years this country has seen unprecedented job loss, especially in the area of manufacturing. As an outplacement consultant, I have worked with thousands of individuals who have been caught up in a downsizing and more times than not they are ready for a job or a career change. Many of them are looking to be challenged, but have not been courageous enough to take the first step.

Ask any human resource professional, recruiter, or hiring manager what they look for in a strong candidate and they will give you a number of varying attributes. Even the process of finding an opportunity and interviewing has changed. The days of applying for a job and getting hired with no interview are long gone. You may find a position through blind luck, but it is indeed a proven fact that your odds are much better if you truly know yourself and your strengths; have a plan; and understand what factors motivate you and make you valuable to a potential employer.

The first step in your search is to develop a job or career objective clearly and accurately describing what you can do for a prospective employer. That objective should reflect your abilities, interests and temperament, as well as your experience. Your job search begins with an honest self-evaluation. You will find that this book will help you in that process.

> *"Change your thoughts and you change your world"*
> —**Norman Vincent Peale**

I:

You Are In the Driver's Seat of Your Career

You Are in the Driver's Seat of Your Career

I OFTEN USE the metaphor of sitting in the driver's seat of your life. Imagine that the car represents your life. First of all, you have to put the key in the ignition and start it. That's a big step. Then, you have to put it in to gear. How many of us have felt like we were sitting in a car just idling, waiting for something to happen? One of my favorite tasks I ask my clients to do is to describe their dream job. This is an integral part of the Career Directioning process. It's truly amazing how many of us either lose sight of what we once planned on doing with our career or, worse yet, cannot even describe what that ideal job would look like. I have spent my career listening to people's dissatisfaction with their jobs and careers. When I ask them what their passion is they often cannot answer. There is a plaque that hangs on the wall in my study and it reads as follows:

> **"It's never to late to become what you might have been"**
>
> —*George Eliot*

I considered naming this section of the chapter "Tell Me about Your Sunday Nights" because I have often heard people describe in agonizing detail how they dread going to work on Monday mornings. Should work be this arduous? In my experience with thousands of individuals who have independently opted to change careers or whose employers have made that decision for them, it has become clear that those who knew their passion and pursued it seemed to be the most content. An effective career development plan is based upon strategy and preparation.

Do you know in what occupation your passions lie? Are you on the right road? Are you living the life that you want? Are you employed in a position that is unfulfilling? Are you looking for a career change? Have you been a victim of downsizing? It has been said that the only true success in life is to have lived life in your own way. Do you feel as though you are just sitting in your career idling? What would life be like if you lived your life in your own way? When was the last time that you thought about it? Did you have a dream like most of us as you were growing up to be or to do something and life got in the way? Wouldn't it be wonderful if you could get up tomorrow and go to work in a position where you would feel as though you are contributing something to the organization? Or being employed where you are appreciated for what you do? Do you feel as though you need to hit the brakes and totally change the direction of your career? Or better yet, work in a position that you know you are making a difference? Life is too short to spend time in a career that is not fulfilling. Too many people ask themselves what kind of job or career would be best for them. Why is it that we focus on the "what" rather than the "how?" Well, it is possible, but you must make it happen. You can't wait for employers to come to you. You have to take charge of the direction of your career direction yourself. What is your rationale for reading this book? Could it be one of the following?

- You are searching for a more satisfying career.
- You have been downsized from a job.
- You are starting you first job search.
- You are feeling your opportunities for growth are limited where you are presently.
- You have a basic conflict of values on the job.
- You are a Baby Boomer and are now seeking a career that you hope will be more satisfying.
- You have experienced a significant life event that is propelling you to make a career change. It could be something like a near death experience, divorce, turning 40 or 50, or physically unable to do the job that you have done in the past.
- You feel as though by changing jobs you will increase your earning power.
- You would like to pursue a dream or complete a mission.
- You were fired or laid off and need to make a career change.
- You have retired and now are seeking a rewarding career that you would enjoy more.
- You have climbed the corporate ladder and your priorities have changed.

Whenever I travel I make a point of asking what people do and how they prepared for their career. I have always been fascinated how people select their career. It is interesting indeed to hear the stories of how Americans manage their careers, or if they really do. Often we allow corporations or organizations to manage our careers. In my private coaching practice I have helped thousands of individuals who have allowed corporations to totally control their lives. When their job was eliminated or the company was acquired by another publicly traded corporation, they found themselves searching for a new direction. Like other career coaches, I feel privileged to help people realize their dreams by showing them the techniques and methods of changing the direction of their career much like a travel agent making suggestions of where to travel and what to see.

> *"Success is not the key to happiness. Happiness is the key to success. If you love what you are doing you will be successful."*
> **Albert Schweitzer**

Being Emotionally Prepared to go Through a Career Transition

GOING THROUGH A career transition can be quite trying; in fact psychologists agree that it ranks almost as high on the stress scale as the death of a loved one. A Swiss psychiatrist and author, Dr. Elisabeth Kubler-Ross, postulated a theory of grieving loss. She had been widely recognized as a foremost authority in the field of death, dying and transition. I have made it a practice to always mention to those individuals who have been the victim of a corporate downsizing the stages of loss. You can be immobilized by fear and discouragement. To an individual who has been downsized, change can be difficult. Are you emotionally prepared for a career change? Let's face it, changing a job by your choice or the end result of someone else's decision can be a traumatic experience. You may experience one or more of the stages listed below.

Denial

Most employees who have been displaced go through this stage of disbelief and shock. Losing your job due to a downsizing, facility closing, or a layoff ranks as one of the most stressful events that can happen in your life. A major automotive manufacturing facility was closing in a Midwestern city where I was working as an outplacement consultant. Much to the surprise of management, the day after the employees were notified of the plant closing, a small contingent of men came to the security gate reporting to work and the security guard had to turn them away. They were in complete denial and could not believe that their employment had been terminated. The security guard explained to them that their jobs no longer existed and sent them anyway. I can recall another man who, once his manager had informed him that his job was being eliminated, immediately spoke up, convinced that his boss was kidding him. Another former client waited an entire week to share with his wife that his company had laid him off. He continued to get up in the morning, going through his normal routine of preparing for the day and heading off to work. He would then come to my office where he would spend the day and return home.

Anger

The next stage in the grieving process is anger. This can be manifested in a number of ways, even toward people who are not involved in the individual's life. A good example might be a person who lost his position to restructuring blowing up at a family member or a good friend over a small matter. People who have been let go by their employer deal with anger issues in a number of ways. They become hostile toward their employer: many companies now have security standing by to deal with the possibility of an enraged employee who has just been informed they have been terminated.

Bargaining

Bargaining is the next stage. I can vividly recall a gentleman who, as the Human Resource professional had just informed him that his job was being eliminated, stated "Look, I will take any job with the company just to get me to retirement, which is only five years away." Who would want to accept employment with a company who has just informed you that your services were no longer needed?

Depression or Sadness

According to Dr. Kubler-Ross, depression or sadness is the next stage. As I mentioned before, grieving the loss of a job can lead to depression. There is a huge difference between someone who is mildly depressed and someone who is totally immobilized due to depression. This stage as well as the anger stage can be particularly dangerous if not dealt with properly. If a person feels as though they are suffering from depression or anxiety over the job loss, then they need to seek medical advice.

Acceptance

The last stage of the grieving process is acceptance and it is by far the most beautiful and welcomed stage. At this stage the individual has accepted the fact that her job at that particular company is no longer needed.

Over the years I have often been asked by some of the people who I have worked with if I felt as though they should still plan on a family vacation that has been scheduled for some time. My response has always been if you feel as though you can afford to spend the money on this vacation, you should absolutely go. What is the difference of a week or two in your job search?

At this point concentrate on taking care of yourself in the following ways:

- You need to stay focused
- Take care of yourself; get plenty of sleep, take vitamins, exercise, etc.
- Do something every day to stay focused on your goal.
- Stay mentally charged
- Think positively

Think of it this way, you are forging ahead in the direction in which you want to travel with your career as you are reading this book. Never forget that you are in the driver's seat of your career.

> *"Our dreams can come true if we have the courage to pursue them."*
> —**Walt Disney**

The Transition Process

The Bridges Transition Model

ACCORDING TO WILLIAM Bridges, a well known speaker, writer and principal of William Bridges and Associates, in order for a person to make a successful career transition they must go through three phases. These phases are Ending, the Neutral Stage, and a New Beginning. They have a natural tendency to overlap.

I. The Ending Phase

First of all, you must end before beginning as the old adage goes. During this period you are in the process of disengaging from where you used to work and acknowledging that you must go on. For some people, this is the most difficult phase. They have grown accustomed to working for the same employer and perhaps doing the same job for a number of years. Here are some of the mentally healthy ways to become engaged in these stages: sending notes to your former associates, saying your good byes, and coming to terms with the reality that this period of your life is now over.

II. The Neutral Zone Phase

During this phase you might find yourself confused or disoriented. You may ask yourself questions like, "What am I going to do?" "How will I find my way?" "What is my purpose in life?" These types of questions are normal. It is advisable to seek out support from family and friends and locate information about opportunities that appeal to you.

III. The New Beginning Phase

In this phase a new sense of direction and purpose emerges. You look to the future with hope and begin to set new goals and challenges. Most people feel as though this phase is by far the easiest once you work your way through the first two.

Ask yourself the following questions at this point:

- Where am I in this process?
- Am I stuck in one of these phases?
- How can I move on?
- What's holding me back?
- What's it going to take to start a new beginning?

II:

Discover What Career Is Best For You

What is the Best Career for You?

AS A CAREER coach I am often asked: "How do I find out what career is best for me?" There are a number of critical factors to be considered. Career Directioning is indeed a lifelong process and will probably change as you grow older.

The Top Ten Important Factors to Consider When Selecting a Career

These are the top ten most important factors to consider when searching for a career that best suits you:

1. **Motivation.** Most career coaches agree that motivation is the most important factor for long term job satisfaction. In other words, you must decide your purpose for getting out of bed and going to work. Some of the typical questions you should ask are:

    *   What are your interests and are they related to your motivation?
    *   What do you get a sense of accomplishment or achievement?
    *   Do you want to have more control over your life?
    *   Is there a natural fit between your personality and a specific career?

2. **Ambitions.** What are your long term goals? Some of the questions that you should ask yourself are:

    *   Is your goal to make a lot of money?
    *   Do you feel as though you need to broaden your career?
    *   Have you ever thought of owning your own business or franchise?

3. **Skills**. Having the proper skills proves to be a key factor for success in finding a satisfying career. Your skills must match the skills needed to do the job. Skills can be acquired by natural ability or by specialized training and education. Ask yourself:

    *   Do you possess the right skill set?
    *   Can you learn the proper skills to do a particular job?

- What type of training is available to prepare you for your next career?
- Do you have the natural ability to learn a particular marketable skill?

4. **Personal Values**. What are your personal values? Our values determine any or all of the following:

- Would your ethics, beliefs, or religion play a major part in your decisions?
- What are your lifestyle requirements?
- Is there a particular type of organization that you want to work for?
- Is it important for you to be employed with people who share the same moral principles and values?

5. **Education and Training**. Various levels of education and training are required for different positions. Ask yourself:

- What is your education level?
- Do you need additional training?
- Do you need specific training?
- Is your education or training adequate for what you are pursuing?

6. **Personality Preferences**. Based upon an assessment such as the Myers-Briggs Temperament Indicator what careers appeal to you?

- Are you introverted or extroverted?
- Do you like and need details, or do you rely on your intuition?
- Do you make your decisions more by thinking or by feeling?
- What is your preference for organizing your life?

7. **Stress level.** How much and what kind of stress are you prepared to live with?

- Do you thrive in a stressful environment?
- Are you absolutely opposed to stress in the workplace altogether?

8. **Location.** Is relocation a big concern?

- Are you able to relocate to a different city or part of the country?
- Is relocation a challenge for family responsibilities?

9. **Preferred Environment.** Have you thought about why type of environment would best suit your needs Think about these questions:

- Are you seeking employment where you have autonomy?
- Would you prefer to work in an office environment?
- Do you want to work outside?

10. **Limitations, Roadblocks, or Detours.** We all have limitations and experience roadblocks or detours. Important points to think about here would be:

- What are your financial commitments and limitations?
- Do you have a physical disability or restriction?

"The future belongs to those who believe in the beauty of their dreams."
                                        —Eleanor Roosevelt

Your Ideal Position (Dream Sheet)

WHEN WAS THE last time that you sat down and dreamt about your ideal position? One of the best ways to determine your real work interests is imagining your ideal job. This is a major part of the Career Directioning process.

1. I want you to dream. List at least five activities, functions, or responsibilities you would like to have in your ideal position. Describe your ideal position for you (including self-employment) even if you are not aware of its existence.

2. What types of activities would you like to avoid in your next career?

3. Describe the most ideal position for you:

4. What limitations would hinder you from landing this new position or performing well?

"Go confidently in the direction of your dreams. Live the life that you've imagined" —**Henry David Thoreau**

The Top Ten Myths about Job Satisfaction

THERE ARE LOTS of myths about job satisfaction. I'd like to debunk some of the more popular ones I've heard.

Myth #1 I will never find my perfect job.

Fact: It takes time think about what you believe will be your perfect job. Think of all of the factors that go in to selecting a pleasing occupation. Jobs have position descriptions, but we each bring definition and meaning to our job. Our job can only be the perfect job only if we feel fulfilled by our intrinsic job needs. For instance, how we feel about what we do or how it relates to our values. Do we need recognition, responsibility or to supervise people? What suits another person may not be our first choice of a job. There are so many factors to be considered such as working conditions, location, values of the company, and salary.

Myth #2 Choosing a career is simple.

Fact: In actuality, choosing a career is an involved and multi faceted process. Developing a career deserves our energy and time. Career planning is an involved process that entails learning about yourself and occupations which you are considering. It's sad to think that most Americans do not devote much time or energy in determining which career would be best for them and their unique gifts, skills, and abilities.

Myth #3 To be totally satisfied, I must change to fit the job.

Fact: While it is true that we often stretch or grow in to a job, some basic skills and abilities are prerequisites for any satisfying position. We must try making the situation and circumstances work in our favor to experience success. In starting a new job, the key word is flexibility. How many times have you heard of a friend or family member landing a new job and then discover the actual responsibilities were completely different from what they thought.

Myth #4 My job must have meaning and purpose.

Fact: Not all jobs have meaning and purpose. What is meaningful to one person will not be so to the next. We define our own job satisfaction based upon our own values, skills, beliefs, and so on. Our job has meaning and purpose only to the extent that we give it meaning and purpose.

Myth #5 I will probably get stuck in an unsatisfying job for the rest of my working life.

Fact: There are more career opportunities available now than ever before. We live in an age in which you can be practically anything you choose or desire. In considering how often corporations and organizations change, it is unlikely that you will stay with the same company for more than just a few years. Most of us will probably have five to seven different types of jobs before reaching retirement age.

Myth #6 I can't make a living by working my hobby.

Fact: It's surprising how often we hear of someone who has taken a hobby and launched it into a satisfying and profitable career. When choosing a career, it makes perfect sense to choose one related to the activities we enjoy in our spare time. Let's face it; we always do better when our hobbies and career fields are a good fit with our skill level. I can think of many of former clients who have decided to follow their heart and open up their own business, whether it is a computer repair business, a music store or purchasing a franchise.

Myth #7 This company offers more money than the other one, so I should be happier.

Fact: A larger salary does not always equate to job-satisfaction. Traditionally the larger the company, the better the salary and benefit packages are more appealing as compared to smaller or medium sized companies. Money does not make for a happy or fulfilling job or career. Think of the people that you know that may make more money than what you have made. Are they any more content than what you are?

Myth #8 I'll find my next position through a headhunter (recruiter).

Fact: Most recruiters only work with you if you are exactly what they are looking for. Remember, companies that rely heavily on recruiters have a screening process; they are looking for ways to disqualify you rather than qualify you for a position. Percentage wise, only about 25% of all of the professional jobs are filled through the use of recruiters. My advice is to limit the number of recruiters to only three. If you use any more it may be hard to keep track of the progress of your job search.

Myth #9 If I go into management I will be happier than if I stay in the technical area.

Fact: Who says you will be happier going in to management? If you are the kind of person who loves the technical aspect of the job, look for an organization that encourages career growth for core technical work and pays a salary at par with a management salary. Besides, management has it own set of challenges that are quite different as compared to staying in a technical, hands on area.

Myth #10 A career coach can tell me what occupation to select.

Fact: While a qualified career coach assists in many ways, such as administering career interest inventories and personality tests, resume advice, interviewing tips and techniques, it is ultimately up to you to decide which job will be the best match.

"Choose a job you love and you will never have to work a day in your life."
                                                                    Confucius

III:

Assess Where You Are

The Myers-Briggs Temperament Indicator ©
Assessment

THERE IS AN entire host of assessments available on the market today to assess all kinds of things. One of the most accurate personality assessment tools is called the Myers-Briggs Temperament Indicator©. The MBTI © has been administered to more than 2 million people and translated in to 16 languages and is the most widely used personality inventory on the market. It helps individuals discover their own personality types while learning about the types of others. The results are powerful once they are understood. You can go online and take this assessment for a nominal fee. You will find it amazingly beneficial in your job search. The MBTI © instrument measures your stated preferences. It is the most widely used personality inventory on the market. It is helpful because it gives you a rational and detached view of yourself as you relate to the world. The MBTI © is based on the insights of Carl Jung. This instrument provides information that allows for a better understanding of your personality type, which can often lead to increased job satisfaction. This helps in identifying job families and occupations that are a good fit based upon your preference type.

The MBTI © instrument describes the eight preferences. The eight Preference terms are as follows:

• Extroversion	• Introversion
• Sensing	• Intuition
• Thinking	• Feeling
• Judging	• Perceiving

1. Are you an introvert or an extrovert? Where do you prefer to get or redirect your energy?

You are an **Extravert** if you have a preference in dealing with people, situations, or things. This is indicated by the letter "E." If you have a preference to expend your energy to deal with, information, explanations, ideas, beliefs, or "the inner world," then your preference is for **Introversion**. This is noted by the letter "I."

2. ***Do you like and need details, or do you rely on your intuition? What is your preference in dealing with information?***

If you are the type of person who prefers dealing with details and facts, then you have a preference for **Sensing**. This is noted by the letter "S."

If, on the other hand you prefer to work with ideas or imagination your preference is for **Intuition**. This is represented by the letter "N."

3. ***Do you make your decisions based more by thinking or by feeling? What is your preference in making decisions?***

If you prefer to decide in a logical, analytical and objective way then your preference is for **Thinking**. The letter "T" represents your preference for solving problems.

If you, however, prefer to decide using your personal values and or beliefs, then you have a preference is for **Feeling**. This is denoted by the letter "F."

4. ***What is your preference for organizing? It could be your job, your workplace, your schedule or your life in general.***

If you prefer your life to be predictable and organized, then your preference is for **Judging**. This is represented by the letter "J."

If you prefer spontaneity and flexibility, handling problems as they appear, you have a preference for **Perception**. This is represented by the letter "P."

The 16 Personality Temperament Indicators Types

WHEN THESE FOUR letters are placed together, you now know your personality type code. There are sixteen combinations.

The 16 different personality type codes

• ISTJ	• ISFJ	• INFJ	• INTJ
• ISTP	• ISFP	• INFP	• INTP
• ESTP	• ESFP	• ENFP	• ENTP
• ESTJ	• ESFJ	• ENFJ	• ENTJ

Now that you know your personality type, it can help you to determine the best fit for certain occupations. The following is a brief description of each of the 16 personality preferences.

ISTJ

ISTJs are bound and determined to do what needs to be done, in the right way, in the right order. They are sometimes called inspectors because they like to ensure all details are taken into account. They know what should be done.

ISTJs have a true sense of what is right and wrong. When they begin the process of making a decision, it is always based upon the details and facts presented. You can always count on ISTJs to be punctual. ISTJs often become frustrated with those who do not follow the rules and are incongruent with their reasoning. ISTJs like to be rewarded for their hard work and due diligence. It is uncomfortable for ISTJs to share their feelings openly. ISTJs prefer working by themselves or in small groups. They look for practical possibilities and consequences on their jobs and off. They enjoy and appreciate organizations that offer security and stability. They are drawn to roles in which they can produce reliability and consistent products or services

Possible career choices for ISTJs:

- Accountant
- Administrator
- Auditor
- Bank Examiner
- Computer Programmer
- Corrections Officer
- Credit Analyst
- Efficiency Expert/Analyst
- Electrician
- Systems Analyst
- General Surgeon
- Government Employee
- Health Care Administrator
- Insurance Underwriter
- Investment Securities Officer
- Lab Technologist
- Legal Secretary
- Library Supervisor
- Math Teacher
- Office Manager
- Physical Education Teacher
- Police Officer / Detective
- School Principal
- Stockbroker
- Technical Writer
- Medical Research
- Computer Specialist
- Government Inspector

ISFJ

ISFJs love to serve others. They are characterized by a strong need to be needed. ISFJs are known as loyal, and at times can be taken advantage of by others who expect them to give. A most common statement made by ISFJs is: "If you want it done right, do it yourself." They love dealing with details. It is no surprise that ISFJs often suffer from psychosomatic illnesses and often feel unappreciated. In the workplace, ISFJs can be counted upon to be methodical and accurate workers. They are very comfortable in one-on-one situations or small groups primarily due to their patience and empathetic approach to others. They like to provide structure for others and they are often taken for granted. ISFJs usually do not choose supervisory roles. ISFJs feel as though they must meet the needs of others. They are great nurturers.

ISFJs have a strong work ethic and their chosen career is important; however you will find their families are the focal point of their lives. They especially enjoy and appreciate working with people who need them. They need time alone to concentrate on solving their problems. ISFJs are loyal to their friends or to a cause and sometimes to a fault. ISFJs seek employment with organizations that offer security, belonging, and loyalty towards others. They feel most comfortable when they can help other people achieve their goals.

Usually; ISFJs only have a few close friends. ISFJs oppose any form of confrontation. They are always ready to provide emotional and practical support to family members and co workers.

Possible career choices for ISFJs:

- Ministry
- Elementary Education
- Nursing
- Social Worker
- Underwriter
- Medicine
- Hospital Administrator
- Religious Work
- Office Manager

- Clerical / Secretarial Work
- Administrative Career
- Broker / Realtor
- Librarian
- Bookkeeper
- Host / Hostess
- Flight Attendant
- Interior Decorators
- Paralegals

ISTP

ISTPs are performers but tend to be mechanically inclined rather than artistic, like those of ISFPs. They seem to save their energy until a project comes along—and then they jump in head first. You can count on them to repair of mechanical challenges.

ISTPs seem to have a need to spread out and have their own space. Under pressure they can react with humor to lessen the tension. They express themselves non-verbally better than verbally. They desire work that they feel is enjoyable and involves a tangible product and will often enjoy making a game out of work.

ISTPs usually have trouble with rote and abstract academic environments; however they are usually exceptional problem solvers in technical areas.

They can be characterized as free spirits. They will often be interested in vocational or technical courses rather than academic college classes and enjoy the tactile approach to occupations. They enjoy a job in which they can be counted on to figure out how things work. ISTPs are exceptional skilled at problem solvers.

Possible career choices for ISTPs:

- Mechanic
- Skilled Trades
- Police Officer
- Emergency Medical
- Chiropractor
- Market Analyst
- Military Personnel
- Intelligence Agent
- Engineer
- Statistician
- Legal Secretary

- Corrections Officer
- Auto Mechanic
- Vocational Technical Instructor
- Engineering Designer
- Inventor
- Paramedic
- Firefighter
- Forensic Pathologist
- Probation Officer
- Landscaper
- Project Manager

ISFP

ISFPs are often known as artists because of their keen sense of awareness of the way things feel, smell, look, and taste. They usually have a strong appreciation for art. ISFPs have a tendency to be reserved and can seem difficult to get to know. They will often stand up for their cause due to their intensely strong sense of values. They possess sensitive souls and have a tremendous capacity for love. They can actually become perfectionists based upon their view of life. They appreciate nature and see beauty in almost everything they encounter.

ISFPs value and accept people for who they are. They believe in unconditional love and truly believe "love is the answer." They usually have a very positive outlook on life and love. They take life very seriously because of their strong sense of values. You will find them most happy and content when their careers allow them the freedom to work toward their personal goals. ISFPs care deeply for other people and recognize the same trait in those that care for them.

They learn best in a kinesthetic or tactile type of learning environment where they can use a hands on approach to a new skill or hobby.

For an ISTP, selecting a career is more like answering a calling. ISFPs are passionate people and have intense feelings. You'll be hard pressed to find a better listener than an ISFP. While they do not have a strong need to manage other people; they often have a strong urge to care for and nurture others.

Possible career choices for ISTPs:

- Child Care Worker
- Carpenter
- Artist
- Firefighter
- Teacher
- Veterinarian
- Musician / Composer
- Designer
- Social Worker
- Psychologist
- Probation Officer
- Engineer
- Computer Specialist
- Athlete
- Paramedics
- Counselor
- Forest Ranger
- Pediatrician

INFJ

Best known as counselors, INFJs are idealists who think and process information abstractly; consequently their feelings and speech help them to achieve their goals. Counselors tend to focus on human potential and are the most empathic of all of the types. Sometimes INFJs are hard to get to know and can appear complicated, but they have the innate capability to relate to complex issues of other people.

INFJs seek careers that allow them to self-actualize. They are a drawn to careers that allow autonomy, variety, and creativity. Their work preference is to help people and utilize theories, ideas, and concepts in human growth. They abhor occupations that concentrate on attention to detail and clerical work.

They rely on their ethical values to make decisions. INFJs have a tendency to be quiet and sensitive. They feel and express their emotions deeply to those who they allow in. Even though INFJs tend to be private and sensitive people, they work intensely with whom they associate with, whether it is friends, coworkers, or family. INFJs can be hurt emotionally rather easily due to their sensitivity

Possible career choices for INFJs:

- Psychology / Counseling
- Priests and Clergy
- Helping Professions
- Biological Scientist
- Mathematician
- College Administrator
- Counselor of Handicapped
- Architect
- Physician
- Psychiatrist
- Educational Consultant
- Spiritual Director
- Psychologist
- Marketing Personnel
- Counselor / Therapist
- College Professor
- Psychiatrist
- Photographer
- Chiropractor
- Musician / Artist
- Educational Consultant
- Missionary

INTJ

INTJs focus internally. Others can view them as being arrogant. INTJs love knowledge and ideas. They enjoy living in an environment of new ideas and like to plan for the future. They respect intelligence and usually have high standards for themselves as well as others. INTJs like to sit back and observe their world and think of possibilities. They are quick to express judgments and tend to have little patience. In a group they are usually the first ones to understand a new concept or way of doing something due to their insight. They are excellent team players if their voices are allowed to be heard.

INTJs see the big picture, they are known as natural leaders. They do not; however have a need to be in the spotlight. They are notorious for being great strategists, whether it is in a military position or in business. You will find that INTJs are self directed, sure of themselves, and excellent strategic thinkers. You find INTJs in engineering or scientific occupations because they have the ability to organize, orchestrate, and plan. They can always be counted upon to improve a project or plan. Sometimes INTJs are misunderstood because they appear to be aloof and quiet. INTJs often are interested in planning and implementing new ideas. They prefer to work by themselves or with a small group. Sometimes other people feel as though INTJs are too rigid and unmovable in their options and strategies.

Possible career choices for INTJs:

- Executive
- Cardiologist
- Scientist
- University Professor
- Physical Scientist
- Technician
- Engineer
- Management
- Psychologist
- Business Analyst

- Computer Specialist
- Researcher
- Administrator
- Photographer
- Lawyer
- Actuary
- Operations Executive
- Business Administrator
- System Analyst
- Researcher

INFP

INFPs need a career in which they help others and truly make a difference. They need to feel a sense of accomplishment in their chosen career. Their lives must have meaning. INFPs enjoy plenty of variety and flexibility, not only in their occupations but in their lives as well. INFPs are adaptable and unlike other personality types because they welcome new concepts, information, and ideas. They enjoy time alone to reflect, plan, and come up with new ideas. They enjoy helping others realize their dream and potential. It has been said that INFPs never lose their sense of wonder of their world.

They value creativity and spirituality. They are not necessarily motivated by money. They enjoy helping and seeing others grow. They do not prefer being associated with bureaucracy.

INFPs look for the good in everything and everyone. INFPs are the individuals who are great to have on a technical team: if something needs to be described without the technical jargon, they are the ones who can pull it off successfully. They do not feel comfortable sharing their deep feelings with others; however, they feel equally at ease working alone or with people.

Possible career choices for INFPs:

- Psychological Fields
- Social Work
- Editor
- Spiritual Work
- Religious Educator
- Journalist
- Psychologist
- Education Consultant
- Social Scientist
- Entertainer
- English Teacher
- Social Worker
- Political Activist
- Counselor
- Psychiatry
- Restaurant Employee
- College Professor
- Art Teacher
- Fine Artist
- Health Officer

INTP

INTPs are analytical people and enjoy problem solving. They may seem to be aloof or detached because their approaches to problems. INTPs correct others without even the slightest hint of realizing what they have done. Normally they are excellent at grammar and learning languages.

INTPs rely on their principles and values and as long as those are not being compromised or violated, they are laid back and easy going. Since they are introverted they don't want to rock the boat, they will often second guess themselves about decisions and fear failure worse than any other type.

INTPs love the challenge of learning a foreign language and the satisfaction of solving a mathematical equation. They are excellent at solving brain teasers and word problems. They are adept at understanding computer systems. INTPs are quite comfortable in careers that provide variety, autonomy, and freedom. If their job is not interesting they will not be very enthusiastic about it. They enjoy learning new, techniques but get bored with administrative responsibilities and routines. Since they love the details they will pick away at all of the possible reasons why something will or will not work. They have a reputation as great thinkers because they ponder the big questions as well as the small. They are drawn to occupations in which they can use their reasoning to solve complex and intellectual problems. The organizations where they seem to flourish are the ones that allow and encourage them to be flexible, unstructured, and autonomous.

Possible career choices for INTPs:

- Staff Development
- Management
- Trainer / Facilitator
- Clergy / Pastor
- Consultant
- Strategic Planner
- College Professor
- Counselor / Therapist
- Lawyer
- Computer Programmer
- Journalist
- Human Resources
- Photographer
- Pharmacist
- Psychologist
- Retailer
- Archaeologist
- Software Designer

ESTP

ESTPs are known by their friends and family to be frank and to the point. Often, they are even calculated risk takers. Their motto is "Just do it." They love to look at life and measure it by the five senses. They view living as one possibility after another and are eager to start on a project rather than ponder the theory behind it. ESTPs make good detectives because of their natural ability to sense little details and pick up on the slightest nuances about people. ESTPs are extremely in tune with others' feelings and attitudes and lean on their improvisation abilities. ESTPs feel no compunction to hide their interests in drama and story telling abilities. They seem to view rules, laws, and regulations as recommendations rather than hard and fast must-dos. They can appear as fast talking persuaders. ESTPs do not trust their instincts very often and can be suspicious of other peoples' intuition because they like to see the facts.

ESTPs look for jobs offering something different every day. They like working with things and people in which they have direct physical contact. They enjoy group processes and dynamics.

ESTPs like to explore experiment and deal with specifics such as engineering and group processes. They make excellent sales people because they improvise along the way. In a classroom setting, the information being presented must be useful to them because if not they easily become bored.

They do not like routine in their lives and are typically excellent entrepreneurs. They possess the ability to motivate others to excitement and action.

ESTPs are fun to be around and are spontaneous. They're enthusiastic and are great motivators. They appreciate working for organizations that allow them flexibility and freedom from the details of day-to-day operations.

Possible career choices for ESTPs:

- Financial Investor
- Small Business Manager
- Export Trade Agent
- Computer Specialist
- Fitness Center Instructor
- Engineer
- International Diplomat
- Tax Investigator
- Community Health Worker
- Police / Detective
- Small Business Manager
- Marketing Personnel

ESFP

ESFPs live in the here and now and their lives are dictated by the five senses. They love to have fun and always seem to have a great time. ESFPs live in the world of people possibilities. They love different types of food, love to meet people and experience all of what life can show them. You will often find that they are the center of attention. ESFPs have very strong inter-personal skills, and frequently find themselves in the role of the peacemaker. ESFPs are quite sensitive to others' feelings and emotions and can be openly empathic. ESFPs are known by being optimistic and quite spontaneous. ESFPs feel as though they are always on stage and ready for the next performance. It seems that everyone likes to be around an ESFP. They generally accept people where and who they are. They are happiest when they are interacting with other people. In general they accept everyone. They are known to be spontaneous but unfortunately seldom plan ahead.

ESFPs are usually very practical, and enjoy going along with the majority and not rocking the boat. They are great team members and team builders. They possess the ability to rally people around a common cause and make it an enjoyable experience. They are kinesthetic learners and learn best when they use their hands rather than reading the directions in completing a task. They do not relish the idea of studying a theory. They take great pleasure in being surrounded by objects of art and appreciate aesthetic beauty.

ESFPs usually like to feel connected with nature. ESFPs are usually a lot of fun to be around and have an appreciation for life. They are excellent at bringing teams together because of their genuine interest in other people.

Possible career choices for ESFPs:

- Human Resources
- Public Relations
- Television / Radio Personality
- Performing Arts
- Elementary Education
- Nursing
- Artist / Actor
- Sales Representative

- Counselor
- Marketing Specialist
- Social Worker
- Fashion Designer
- Performer
- Interior Decorator
- Consultant
- Photographer

ESTJ

The motto of an ESTJ is always "What you see is what you get." They are straightforward in their approach to others. They measure life by the five senses because they like to deal with situations in a rational and logical way. ESTJs always want the facts. They are practical and dependable. They live their lives by a set of beliefs and standards. If you want a job done and done right call on an ESTJ. ESTJs are usually very verbal and rarely have problems expressing themselves. They make excellent leaders mainly because of their innate ability to see the goal and then work toward achieving it. You will find them to be aggressive and self-confident. ESTJs are take-charge people. They are known as some of the most conscientious of all of the types. ESTJs like to express themselves and can, at times, be demanding and critical. ESTJs can be loud and the center of attention at parties. ESTJs have a tendency to be too rigid at times and can become overly detail-oriented. Under stress, an ESTJ can feel isolated from others, misunderstood, and undervalued.

ESTJs are known a "joiners." They are attracted to joining organizations such as Boy Scouts or the PTA, or even their local homeowners association. This is because they feel an obligation to support the community or the goals of society at large. They have a sense of duty in their lives, whether it is in their occupations, their relationships, or even their community.

Possible career choices for ESTJs:

- Military Leader
- Business Administrator
- Police / Detective Work
- Business Manager
- Lawyers / Judge
- Financial Officer
- Business Manager
- High School Teacher
- Government Employee
- Politician
- Security Guard
- Religious Educator
- Administrator
- Social Worker
- Insurance Agent
- Technical Teacher
- Sales Representative
- Not for Profit Professional
- Business Manager
- Plant Manager
- Union Leader
- Nursing Administrator

ESFJ

Whenever discussing ESFJs, the single word that comes to mind is guardian. They are guardians in every sense of the word. They like and honor traditions. ESFJs work hard and play hard. They enjoy meeting and interacting with people; face-to-face cooperative work that provides practical service to people.

ESFJs usually enjoy being in charge and are excellent at delegating. They will often see problems clearly and quickly. Because of the "F" in their type ESFJs can be sensitive to what others say or do to them. They can become excellent actors and actresses because of this ability to feel their part. Out of all of the preference types ESFJs have the greatest sense of right and wrong; however, they also have a nurturing side that likes to rescue others. They assume responsibility for the welfare of others. They are loyal and sensitive to the needs of others. ESFJs seek careers that provide a lot of contact and interaction with people. They want to help, care for and nurture people. They are happiest when they have clearly defined roles that have visible and measurable results. They like to be assured they are useful, needed, and wanted. They need personal feedback on their contributions.

As caretakers, ESFJs sense danger and can best be described as vigilant. They are exemplary in the role of a protector, such as those in the medical and elementary education fields. They are drawn to careers that involve gathering, recording, retrieving and storing of detailed information that is related to people. They are excellent team players and if on a sales team, they will always watch out for the interests of the customer.

Possible career choices for ESFJs:

- Host / Hostess
- Social Worker
- Elementary School Teacher
- Medical Assistant
- Physician
- Public Relations
- Dental Assistant
- Marketing Director
- Real Estate Sales

- Receptionist
- Sales Professional
- Organization Leader
- Religious Educator
- Sales Clerk
- Child Care Worker
- Flight Attendant
- Sales Manager
- Nursing Home Administrator

ENFP

ENFPs can be characterized as those who come up with great ideas and feel very comfortable around others. ENFPs have such great charm that they easily can persuade others to their point of view. They love people and people are drawn to them. They are easy lovers; they enjoy showing affection and tenderness. They can use their polished social skills to persuade people to their side of opinions. They are known to be affectionate; however, their attention span in relationships can be short. You will find ENFPs to be easygoing, and enjoyable to work with. You can count on them to come up with great ideas; however, they have a tendency to get bored quickly. They can also have a tendency to put off tasks that entail details. ENFPs usually work well with "Js" because they recognize the fact that they need to be kept on track. ENFPs are not comfortable in a bureaucracy.

ENFPs can go from being very serious to just plain silly in a flash. What strikes ENFPs as hilarious may not strike others humorous at all. ENFPs have a natural ability to role play and have a personality for drama and acting. Friends are very important to ENFPs. They will hold up their end of the relationship, sometimes at the sake of being victimized by others. ENFPs are energized by being around people. Some ENFPs have difficulty being alone and can find it stressful.

Possible career choices for ENFPs:

- Actor / Actress
- Musician
- Social Worker
- Therapist
- Advertising Account Executive
- Career Counselor
- Management Consultant
- Magazine Reporter
- Graphics Designer

- Art Director
- Copy Writer
- Corporate Trainer
- Psychologist
- Human Resources
- Child Welfare Counselor
- Diplomat
- Television reporter
- Journalist

ENTP

ENTPs have a reputation for being clever. They can process several ideas simultaneously while still being in the present moment. A good example is the salesmen that can multi process several big sales deals and yet appear to be in the present moment when speaking to a new client. ENTPs are notorious for quick thinking and often are known as being ingenious at solving problems.

They are usually quite competitive and love a challenge. Even though ENTPs are optimists more times than not, they still can come up with an argument quicker than most in the crowd.

ENTPs like to bond with their loved ones. ENTPs like to hang out with friends who are sharp and entertaining, they can become bored with people who are not with it. They feel fulfilled when they find a career in which they can express their creativity.

Possible career choices for ENTPs:

- College Professor
- Management Consulting
- Food Service Workers
- Tax Investigator
- Radiology Technologist
- Computer Analyst
- Sales Representative
- Financial Investor
- Dietetic Researcher
- Entrepreneur
- Investment Banker

- Lawyer
- Credit Investigator
- Psychologist
- Marketers
- Computer Programmer
- Journalist
- Writer
- Politician
- Entrepreneur
- Inventor
- Business Manager

ENFJ

ENFJs have charisma. People are naturally drawn to them because they sense a genuine interest and caring. They are dreamers and love to help others realize their full potential. They often make excellent entrepreneurs. They intuitively know and understand others' needs. In fact, they tend to define life in the context and priorities of the needs of others. They are creative and imaginative; however, they are extremely sensitive to criticism and discord. Even though they show their emotions, their friends want to open themselves up and talk about the deeper issues in their lives. They often make excellent therapists or counselors, but have the potential to get too involved emotionally with the client. Given the right circumstances, they can provide excellent leadership.

ENFJs appreciate people. They are often known as givers. Sometimes you will find ENFJs to be promoters or persuaders. They have an innate ability to connect with others. They are at risk for being hurt or even abused by less sensitive people. ENFJs often take on burdens of others more than they care to bear. ENFJs have tremendous communication and interpersonal skills. It has been said that they possess the gift of encouragement.

Possible Career choices for ENFJs:

- Consultant
- Psychologist
- Social Worker
- Counselor
- Teacher
- Clergy
- Career Counselor
- Writer
- Sales Representative
- Facilitator
- Human Resources Manager
- Manager
- Events Coordinator
- Sales Representative
- Politician
- Diplomat
- Marketing Specialist
- Artist / Actor
- Trainer
- Religious Worker
- Project Manager
- College Professor

ENTJ

You can often tell an ENTJ by their natural tendency to command or direct a group of people. They have a natural tendency to direct people. They possess charm and finesse. The ENTJ requires no encouragement to develop a plan, they do however value knowledge. It seems that ENTJs are often "larger than life." This is because they have the drive, the persuasive ability, and personality to make big things happen. They have a natural propensity to be great storytellers or salesmen.

ENTJs see what needs to be done, and have an extraordinary sense of knowing who would be best at achieving the goal of the group. They have an unusual ability to marshal people together to accomplish what needs to be done. If you need a project completed ask an ENTJ. They enjoy occupations that allow them to plan and research. They will not waiver in their resolve.

Possible career choices for ENTJs:

- Human Resources
- Designer
- Project Manager
- Manager
- Marketing Specialist
- Consultant
- Academic Lecturer
- Public Relations
- Lawyers
- Entrepreneur
- University Professor
- Organization Founder
- Mortgage Banker
- Scientist
- Teacher
- Psychologist
- Computer Systems Analyst
- Administrative Manager
- Bank Manager
- Stockbroker
- Environmental Planner
- Economist
- Curriculum Designer
- International Banker
- Technical Trainer
- Mortgage Broker
- Franchise Owner
- Pharmaceutical Sales

Personal Values Assessment

WHAT ARE YOUR work values? Studies have consistently shown that people who work in fields that mirror their values are much more satisfied with their chosen occupation. If their basic values are not aligned, then there is a greater chance for discontent.

Directions: This exercise is designed to help you identify your particular work values. Below you will find a list of various work values. Place a check mark to the right of each value important to you.

When thinking about the activities in which you engage while working, what seems to be most satisfying to you?

Physical activity   _____
Variety   _____
Analyzing   _____
Contact with public   _____
Problem solving   _____
Taking a risk   _____

What values are imperative to you in your working environment?

Laid back environment   _____
Autonomy   _____
High salary   _____
Location   _____
Quiet work environment   _____

What seems to be the biggest motivators on the job for you?

Sense of pride   _____
Power or influence   _____
Community   _____
Sense of belonging   _____
Status   _____
Responsibility   _____

What are your values as they relate to the interaction you have with others on the job?

Teamwork	_____
Managing others	_____
Cooperation	_____
The care of others	_____
Being recognized	_____

Personality Preference Assessment

OUR PERSONALITY PREFERENCES are as unique to us as our fingerprints. Tasks that come easily to some people may not come easily to others. For instance, conducting a training session or teaching a class seems second nature to those who are good at it and enjoy it. While others would rather spend time by themselves, crunching numbers on a computer in a cubicle. This exercise helps us discern our personality preferences. There are two columns listed below. As you make your choice remember there isn't one that that is any better or worse than the other. They simply are different behaviors or personality characteristics.

Directions: Circle the personality preferences that best describes you:

Cooperative	Inquisitive
Diplomatic	Competitive
Spontaneous	Predicable
Cooperative	Methodical
Detail-oriented	Concept or idea-oriented
Organized	Flexible
Calm, peaceful	Driven
Calculated	Flexible
Creative	Independent
Responsible	Passionate
Black and white thinker	Negotiator
Researcher	Active listener
Adaptive	Independent
Optimistic	Rigid thinker
Strategic thinker	Tactical thinker
Big picture thinker	Minute detailer
Logical thinker	Sensitive to people
One task at a time	Multi-task
Team player	Team leader

In the space below list any other unique personality characteristics that best describe you:

_____

_____

_____

At this point, take a look at the words that are circled above. What do they tell you about your particular personality? If you have been honest with yourself, you can understand these parts of who you are and can find a position utilizing your unique personality, thusly giving you greater satisfaction with your career.

Abilities Assessment

DO YOU KNOW what your natural abilities are and how have you used them in the past? Do you feel comfortable getting up in front of a crowd to make a presentation or do you enjoy researching? Are you gifted in the areas of listening, relating and counseling others when they describe what is happening to them?

According to employer surveys across the country, the inability to effectively communicate what your skills are is the number one problem of job seekers. Have you thought about your natural abilities or skills? Can you articulate them effectively?

Directions: Circle the abilities that you feel you possess from the list below:

Planning	Computer Skills
Mechanical Ability	Listening
Leadership	Artistry
Training	Teamwork Building
Organizing	Adaptable
Project Orientated	Written Communication
Negotiating	Verbal Communication
Problem Solving	Interpreting
Flexibility	Coaching
Teaching	Understanding Systems
Memorization	Attention to Detail
Innovation	Imagination
Tenacity	Mathematics
Prioritizing	Follow Through
Facilitating	Sales Presentations
Prioritizing	Persuasion
Research	Big Picture Thinker
Sequential Thinking	Discernment

Developing a Career Strategy

AT THIS POINT think about how your MBTI preference compliments your values, personality preferences and your abilities. Do you see a thread of commonality? Are you pursuing a job that will utilize your MBTI preference, values, personality preferences and your abilities? If so, then you are on your way to your Career Directioning. List in the diagram below your preferences:

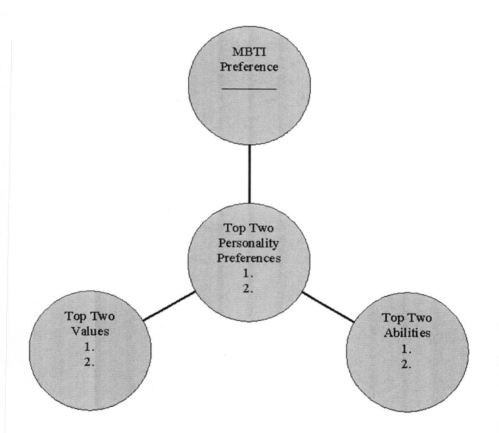

IV:

Resume Development

Your Resume—It's All About Marketing

WHAT ARE THE purposes of a resume? The main purpose of a resume is to promote yourself. Your resume is your marketing tool. Think of it as your sales brochure. It is a document unlike any other document you will ever use in your life. You *must* have a powerful resume. A resume should sell you to the reader. This written presentation is not only who you are but what you are looking for. Most importantly it must say who you are. Another purpose of a resume is to use it as a networking tool. Whenever you are meeting a potential network contact you should be prepared to give them a copy of your resume. This way they will have something to take with them to remember who you are and what you are looking for. You don't staple it, you really shouldn't fold it, and it should be on quality paper of certain colors. Too often people think that once they assemble the facts and details about their work history they will have the "ideal" resume, and will start receiving job offers. It is not that simple. It represents you and your work history, but it should also be a sales brochure on what career related accomplishments you have had so far in your career. More importantly, it should explain how your past accomplishments indicate how you could help the organization where you are applying. It should highlight your accomplishments to show a potential employer your qualifications for the work you want; it is not a biography of everything you have done including unrelated activities. For instance, if you apply for a position in the area of management, it would be totally unrelated and therefore useless to highlight the fact that you have just passed the real estate exam. Why would you want to put it on your resume because it is unrelated to the area that you are pursuing? The sole purpose of a resume is to secure an interview. Your resume should be reflective of more than just your paid work experience, it should also contain details about your volunteer experience as well as any leadership positions that you have held.

Sometimes people say they want their resume to be unique and stand out from others. While that sounds like a good strategy, in actuality if it is too extraordinary you probably will not be considered for the interview. I can think of only one exception to the rule, a young man that I was working with years ago. He was very gifted and quite resourceful. He came up with the idea of folding his resume into the shape of a paper airplane. Then, he folded his cover letter, which was only one half of the size of a regular sized sheet of paper and attached it to the top of the paper airplane along with a note to the recipient that read "Open me first." After that, he very carefully placed it in a shoe box and sent it to an ad agency. The moment that they received it they were on the phone asking him when he could come in for an interview, which ultimately resulted in a job offer and subsequent position. The reason why I highlight this story is to show that sometimes you have to be creative. In this young man's life he had been employed in the creative services field and it was an appropriate strategy. This was quite extraordinary indeed.

You must be knowledgeable about every detail on your resume. That probably seems like a strange statement to make, but I've heard of embarrassing situations in which applicants have made a faux pas. In one example, a candidate interviewed with the hiring manager. The interviewer asked the person to elaborate on the details of his experience; his resume stated that he wrote the human resources handbook for his previous company. Little did the candidate know the interviewer was a good friend of the HR manager at that company. So after the interview was over, he called his friend and inquired if this candidate had, in fact, rewritten the HR manual. As it turned out, he only assisted with the rewrite. Even an exaggeration can be discovered, making you look foolish and desperate.

Summary or Objective Statement?

A COMMON QUESTION that is asked of me is when should a person use a Summary statement as compared to an Objective statement on their resume. The best way to answer that question is to ask yourself the following questions:

- Is your background and work experience in a variety of different fields and different types of experiences? If so, then it is probably best to use the Summary statement. The rationale is because it is demonstrating that you have skills in a variety of areas.
- Are you just entering the job market with limited job experience? Or, are seeking a different career than what you have done previously? Or, perhaps you have been employed in the same field for a long time. If these questions apply, then it is probably best to use an Objective statement.

In my opinion, it's better to use a Summary statement rather than an Objective statement. Here is why. When a person reads an objective statement, that you have listed on your resume it leads them on a particular path. Whereas, if you describe who you are, where you have been, and your qualifications it paints a better overall picture of what you have to offer. For instance, Objective statements often read like this: "Seeking a challenging and responsible position where proven skills will be used to support the overall goals of an organization." Well, I would hope that you would want to be accomplishing that by the very submission of your resume for the job! Compare that Objective statement with this Summary statement. "A professional Financial Advisor with over 10 years of progressive experience with a Fortune 500 company." Do you see the difference? The Summary is much more definitive in nature and informs the reader who you are, at what level that you have been employed, and for the length of time.

Here are a few examples of Summary statements with skills or strengths listed as well:

Experienced Quality Assurance Manager with a broad range of accomplishments in two different types of manufacturing settings. Proven ability to organize projects with available resources to achieve corporate goals.

Areas of Specialty:

• Strategic Planning	• Multimeters
• Supervision	• Engineering Drawings
• QS9002 / ISO 9002	• Team Building Skills

Over 10 years of experience in the area of Social Welfare. Possess a Masters in Social Work and qualifications to administer and interpret several assessments. Particular areas of strengths:

• Project Management	• Interpersonal Communications
• Facilitation Skills	• Analyzing Client Needs

Basic Resume Dos and Don'ts

ALWAYS USE THE active voice on your resume. Notice the different of the following two sentences "Was assigned to a project where the revenue increased significantly" A better way to convey this achievement would be to state it like this: "Managed a team that developed new markets and increased revenues for the department by 60% in less than one year."

Use a professional sounding email address. I worked with an executive once that had an email that read *ohiofarmer@hotmail.com*. Can you imagine the image that would portray? I urged him to change his email to something more conservative.

Never include the following, why you left you last job, salary information, or references. We will discuss the reference sheet later. I am often asked "How long should the resume be?" As rule of thumb, if you have less than 10 or 12 years of work experience then you should be able to articulate what it is that you have done on one page. If, on the other hand, you have had more experience than you want the prospective employer to be aware of, two pages would be apropos. If you are applying for an academic position, a curriculum vita would probably be longer than the standard two page resume due to publications and articles written.

It is advisable to use action words on your resume. I have listed below some words that can help describe or develop accomplishments and achievements. It demonstrates the skills you utilized on the job.

achieved	accomplished	authored	acquired	dministrated
analyzed	activated	approved	arranged	built
budgeted	clarified	completed	composed	conceived
conducted	consulted	controlled	created	delivered
designed	developed	directed	doubled	earned
edited	eliminated	engineered	enhanced	established
evaluated	expanded	facilitated	formed	founded
generated	headed	implemented	improved	increased
initiated	innovated	instituted	integrated	introduced
invented	launched	led	managed	marketed
modified	motivated	negotiated	organized	pioneered
planned	prepared	presented	produced	promoted
proposed	recommended	recruited	reduced	redesigned
reorganized	resolved	restructured	revised	Saved

scheduled	selected	serviced	simplified	sold
solved	started	streamlined	structured	succeeded
supervised	systemized	tracked	trained	transformed
translated	upgraded	utilized	visualized	wrote

Conversely, there are words and phrases you should be cautions of because they are overused and have become cliché. If you decide to use them, be certain you can back up what you are saying. Have an accomplishment prepared to use as an example for each.

- Team player
- Resourceful
- Responsible
- Independent
- Organized
- Sequential Thinker
- Self starter
- Assertive
- Systematic
- Flexible

- Out-of-box-thinker
- Detail oriented
- Motivated
- Knowledgeable
- Organized
- Self motivated
- Creative
- Professional
- Efficient
- Goal oriented

The Top Ten Typical Resume Mistakes

A COMPANY'S FIRST impression of you is your resume. A page or two of that includes your work and educational history and your skills. You must convey important information, be brief and efficient to make a favorable impression.

Mistake # 1: Writing your resume listing only a series of job descriptions.

Give the reader an idea of what you have done throughout your career, do not focus solely on the duties you were responsible for at your previous jobs. List your accomplishments along with quantifiable facts to back up your claims. Saying you were responsible for a 40% growth in overall sales is much more impressive than simply stating you managed a sales team.

Mistake # 2: Writing in the first person.

Your resume should not be written in the first person. Avoid words such as "I" "my" and "me." Use the first person pronouns on your cover letter.

Mistake # 3: Including unrelated and personal information.

Always ask yourself, "Is this related to the position I'm applying for?" Leave out the details about your personal life, marital status, hobbies, and other interests.

Mistake # 4: Using passive language.

Your resume needs to make a strong statement, and one of the ways to do this is by utilizing action words to describe your accomplishments or achievements. Words like "achieved," "developed" "managed," and "implemented" will give your resume a sparkle and make it more interesting to the reader.

Mistake # 5: Repetitiveness.

While it is important to use action words, it's just as important to think about each and every word on your resume. Don't use a couple of words throughout the entire resume. Use your thesaurus if you find you are lacking vocabulary words that help to describe what you are attempting to say.

Mistake # 6: Using "flashy" formatting.

While the most important part of your resume is the content, the overall look and feel is also imperative. Keep your resume simple, bold, and professional. Always use consistent formatting for headings and bullet points. In the same way, steer clear of flashy formatting, unconventional fonts or graphics, unless you seek a highly creative position.

Mistake # 7: Sending a resume without a cover letter.

Always send a cover letter with your resume. Never assume that they will somehow know for which position you are applying. The company or organization could have multiple job openings. A cover letter informs them of which job you'd like to have.

Mistake # 8: Sending a generic resume.

While your past experience does not change with the job or industry you target, your resume certainly should. If you are seeking a sales-related position, your resume will include details different from those included in a resume for a management job.

Mistake # 9: Typos and other spelling or grammatical errors.

Before you send out your resume, make sure you have proofread it several times. If a typo or misspelling is found, many hiring managers will not give a resume a second look and automatically toss it.

Mistake # 10: Sending your resume to a nameless, faceless person.

One sure-fire way to exclude your resume from the stack considered for the job is to send it to the "Hiring Manager" or worse yet, "To Whom It May Concern." Do your homework and ascertain the name (correctly spelled) and title of the Human Resource person. In this day and age, access to the Internet gives little excuse for not locating the name of the HR person at any company.

The Top Ten Phrases That Can Hurt Your Résumé

BE VERY CAREFUL of the words and phrases used on your resume. There are certain words that have a way of diminishing the overall effectiveness of what you are trying to communicate. It sounds great to have a strong work ethic and ambitious, right? Well, you can impress the hiring manager if you can supply specific examples to substantiate your claims.

Some examples are listed below.

1. **Phrase 1:** "Detailed oriented"

   Write this instead: "Maintained a 100% accuracy rate for over two years in the shipping and receiving area."

2. **Phrase 2:** "Team player with self-directed focus"

   Write this instead: *"Collaborated with all members of the cross functional team and achieved results that were exemplary."*

3. **Phrase 3:** "Experienced in working in a multi tasking environment"

   Write this instead: *"Managed a production operation and had P & L responsibilities."*

4. **Phrase 4:** "Excellent written communication skills."

   Write this instead: *"Wrote a training manual that was adopted for use corporate-wide."*

5. **Phrase 5:** "Excellent customer service skills."

   Write this instead: *"Have a reputation for consistently receiving favorable comments"* or *"Developed a customer survey that was utilized as a management tool."*

6. **Phrase 6:** "Excellent work ethic."

   Write this instead: *"Have always exceeded corporate expectations in sales quotas."*

7. **Phrase 7:** "Aggressive and competitive."

   Write this instead: *"Increased sales by 78% in less than 18 months."*

8. **Phrase 8:** "Innovative and creative."

   Write this instead: *"Created a new spreadsheet for all of the accounting departments that resulted in a saving of time and energy."*

9. **Phrase 9:** "Have a take charge personality."

   Write this instead: *"Restructured company to improve performance of profit centers while reducing overhead and operating costs."*

10. **Phrase 10:** "Well organized."

    Write this instead: *"Have the ability to prioritize tasks to be accomplished."*

Career Related Achievement or Accomplishment Statements

ANOTHER QUESTION ASKED regarding resumes is: "How important are achievement statements to the reader?" I cannot emphasize enough the importance of achievement statements. It demonstrates to the reader that the applicant has gone above and beyond all expectations at their previous job. Think back to all you accomplished in the various positions you've held. Now, think how you feel about them. Are you proud of that them? Did it give you a sense of achievement? Only by reviewing our accomplishments can we see how successfully we've used our skills. Realizing how we felt or how others were impacted is the biggest benefit to reviewing our accomplishments.

Only by reviewing past accomplishments and achievements can one be certain if he or she is headed in the right direction. Let me give you an example of what I mean. While working with a client, she described her exuberance for a particular accomplishment. When I asked her what skills she utilized to achieve that accomplishment, she had to stop and think about it. She used her analytical and problem solving abilities in solving a problem for the company that she had been with for some time. It struck me as odd because it was one of her strengths, yet she never really thought of it as a transferable skill. Do you know what your skills are?

The Top 10 Questions to Ask Regarding Your Career Related Achievements:

1. What was the achievement?

2. What kind of actions did you take to achieve it?

3. How does it exemplify your talents?

4. What particular skills did you use?

5. How did the accomplishment highlight my skills and areas of expertise?

6. What were the results?

7. How did the company benefit?

8. How many people were involved in the project?

9. How much money was involved or saved as a result?

10. Why do you think that it was a significant accomplishment?

"What lies behind us and what lies before us are tiny matters compared to what lies within us."   **—Ralph Waldo Emerson**

(Career Related Achievement or Accomplishment Statements Worksheet)

LIST YOUR TOP ten career related achievements or accomplishments you have experienced. They should be related to what you have achieved on the job. As you list them, make a note of the abilities used—your personality traits or preferences—and how your values played a role in its success. Do not be surprised if there is a direct and strong correlation between all of these traits and your successes.

Accomplishment   Abilities   Personality Trait(s)   Values

1. _____

2. _____

3. _____

4. _____

5. _____

6. _____

7. _____

8. _____

9. _____

10. _____

The Top Ten Items to Check on Your Resume Before Submitting It:

1. Is it the best marketing brochure for you?

2. Is the resume focused on what the reader is looking for?

3. Does it include relevant and specific information about the level of responsibility of the positions you have held?

4. Is proper terminology used when describing what you have done and where you were employed?

5. Does each item on your list of strengths tie into an accomplishment somewhere in the resume?

6. Is the language chosen professional, precise and easy to read?

7. Have you begun every accomplishment with an action word?

8. Do your job descriptions focus on the major tasks for which you were responsible, leaving out extraneous details?

9. Are you staying away from ambiguous words so that your resume reads smoothly?

10. Have you checked and rechecked your grammar, spelling, and punctuation?

Volunteer or Community Activities Experience

YOUR VOLUNTEER EXPERIENCE should be added to your resume only if it supports your job objective or demonstrates skills highlighted under your Professional Experience. If your volunteer experience has been limited to membership without holding any officer positions, then perhaps it is best to list it under Associations or Community Activities.

Some organizations such as banking, real estate, and others, being a member of the Rotary, Kiwanis, or the local Chamber of Commerce would be beneficial to list on your resume. Involvement in fundraising for organizations like United Way, American Heart Association, or American Cancer Society could relate. It shows that you have donated your time and efforts for worthy causes and you have developed a network of associates. In fact, a very good friend of mine, who was on a board with me years ago, ended up becoming director of that organization due to his involvement on the board. So never underestimate all of the positives that can accompany your involvement in community activities and always add them to your resume.

Which Resume Format is Best for You— Chronological or Functional Format?

THERE ARE TWO basic resume formats to choose from, the chronological and the functional. Each has its own particular strong points. The chronological format is the most common type of resume. It lists the job titles and responsibilities, starting with the most recent position held and working backwards. If you are looking to highlight how you have grown and accepted more responsibilities over the years, this is probably the best resume format for you. The chronological formatted résumé is by far the most preferred; in fact, most human resource professionals and hiring managers prefer to see a chronological résumé. The chronological formatted resume states a Summary or Objective statement first. Then, it goes on to list the employers that you have been employed by with the most recent employer listed first. It then describes your education and related training and finally any community activities.

Whereas if you prefer to use the Functional formatted resume then it would look like this. You would list your Summary or Objective, just like the Chronological resume. Then it would discuss your skills in various areas, such as Marketing, Sales, etc. Then it lists your employers and finally your education and Community activities. If you use a functional format you might be sending the wrong signal. If, however, you are just graduating from school and have limited experience, this may not, be the best way to go. It starts out by listing your work experience in reverse chronological order and perhaps without dates. The emphasis here is on areas of responsibility and listing significant accomplishment.

A functional formatted resume is one that highlights the skills you have obtained over the years. The best part of a functional resume is how it downplays your job titles and promotes your greatest skills. Knowing employers prefer the chronological formatted resume, it is with caution that you use this format. The functional formatted resume is usually best for your first resume right out of school. The rationale behind it is you most likely do not have work experience. I usually recommend someone use this format of resume if they are in any of the following categories:

- You have been with the same company for a number of years.
- You are in the process of changing careers.
- There have been gaps in your employment.
- You are a recent college graduate with limited work experience.

- You have been away from the work place for a while.
- You have had a number of short term assignments with different companies.

I have included a few samples of functional resumes later in the chapter.

"Whatever you are, be the best you can be." —Abraham Lincoln

(Chronological Resume Format Worksheet)

Name _____

Address _____

City, State, Zip _____

Phone / Fax _____

Email _____

SUMMARY (or) OBJECTIVE

_____
_____
_____

WORK EXPERIENCE

Name of Company (most recent employer) _____

Location _____

Dates of Employment (years only) _____

Job Title and primary responsibilities

_____
_____
_____

Accomplishments (highlighting your skills)

_____
_____
_____
_____
_____

Name of Company _____

Location _____

Dates of Employment (years only) _____

Job Title and primary responsibilities

_____

_____

_____

Career Related Accomplishments (highlighting your skills)

_____

_____

_____

_____

_____

Name of Company _____

Location _____

Dates of Employment (years only) _____

Job Title and primary responsibilities

_____

_____

_____

Accomplishments (highlighting your skills)

_____

_____

_____

_____

_____

EDUCATION

University / College (highest degree received) _____

Location _____

Dates _____

Degree Earned _____

University / College (highest degree received) _____

Location _____

Dates _____

Degree Earned _____

COMMUNITY ACTIVITIES (or) AFFILITATIONS

(Example—Chronological Resume)

DIANE BARRIS-THOMPSON

98278 East Pikeville Lane Chicago, IL 68298
512.398.2980 ~ mkdonahugh@hotmail.com

OBJECTIVE

Seeking an opportunity where experience in the printing industry along with
proven supervisory abilities to motivate employees will be utilized.

EXPERIENCE

Freeflow Industries, Chicago, IL   2001-Present

Production Manager
Responsibilities included overseeing all of the printing operations to include
raw materials, machine maintenance, personnel supervision and shipping.

- Increased production of all machines by 49%.
- Cut overall costs of the department by 27% in less than one year.
- Developed a five-year business plan that has helped senior management
  in their goals and objectives.

Barnes & Barney Printing, DeKalb, IL1   996-2001

Supervisor
Duties entailed managing the print operation of the company and had
responsibility for budget and advertising. Had oversight for all production and
shipping.

- Managed 12 people in the department.
- Proposed a new procedure that ultimately resulted in saving time and
  material.
- Developed an innovative method that improved the company image.

DIANE BARRIS-THOMPSON

Page—2

Dominic's Printing, Chicago, IL   1993-1996

Printing Manager

Had overall responsibilities for every facet of the printing operation, to include budget, staffing, and production.

- Increased production by 39% in the first year of the position.
- Improved the accuracy of customer orders drastically.
- Cut waste by 12% by introducing a new method of cleaning the printing presses.

EDUCATION

A.S., Business Technology, Calumet Community College, Calumet, IL

(Example—Chronological Resume)

DAVID LLEWELLYN
9820 West Washington Blvd.
Fort Worth, TX 78309-3982
(512) 398-2980
dlou@yahoo.com

SUMMARY

Skilled professional salesman with the ability to persuade the customer to make the right choice about a product or service. Have over 10 years of experience in retail promotion programs with successful launches of new products.

PROFESSIONAL EXPERIENCE

Zackery Sales, Connersville, TX   2000-Present

Sales Promotion Manager

Have full range of responsibilities that include: planning, budgeting, and implementation of all new products.

- Increased market share by 73% in less than 3 years.
- Negotiated the biggest sale for he company ever, $2M.
- Successfully launched three new products lines.
- Managed a $140K promotion budget.

Beautiful Teeth Products, San Antonio, TX   1993-2000

Product Promotion Manager

Responsibilities included all retail promotion programs in the dental area of available products. Developed promotional items for tradeshows and exhibits as well as advertising sales materials, pricing, sales objectives, and all new products. Traveled extensively promoting products to distributors and retailers.

- Successfully introduced a new product that netted a profit of more than $78K.

DAVID LLEWELLYN **Page—2**

- Established the first ever council on marketing and sales for the company.
- Launched a campaign ad that proved to be one of the most successful campaigns in the company's history.
- Was promoted to Product Promotion Manager within the first six months on the position.

All State Insurance, San Antonio, TX 1988-1993

Insurance Salesman

Managed a district office with 6 professionals. Sold life, casualty and automotive insurance. Was responsible for all sales promotions, advertising, staffing, and budgeting. Other activities included training and product positioning

- Successfully set up 26 new offices in the region.
- Established a presence in the area.
- Exceeded all sales expectations for the first three consecutive years.

EDUCATION

MBA, Concentration in Marketing, Michigan State, Lansing, MI (GPA 3.97/4.0)
B.S., Business Administration, North Carolina State, High Point, NC
A.S., General Business, San Antonio College, San Antonio, TX

COMMUNITY AFFILIATIONS

Volunteer—American Cancer Society
Board Member—Boy Scouts of America
Volunteered—Make-A-Wish Foundation
Executive Board Member—Big Brothers Big Sisters

(Example—Chronological Resume)

Brent J. Berger
1298 Avalon Way
Fort Worth, TX 46825
512/903-9236
brentjberger7@hotmail.com

Professional Profile

A successful manager of resources. Conscientious team player with hands on project management experience along with demonstrated strengths in planning, and organization. Possess the ability to improve and adapt quickly to changes in the workplace environment.

Areas of Expertise

- Communication Skills
- Problem Solving
- Marketing and Sales
- Relationship Management
- Operations

- Persuasion Skills
- Teamwork Building
- Attention to Detail
- Quality Control
- Human Resource

Professional Experience

MERIDIAN MUTUAL INSURANCE COMPANY, Antwerp, TX   2004-Present

Project Manager
Responsible for the management of staff, facilities, budget and overall operations of the underwriting department. Manage a staff of six professionals and three admin personnel.

- Streamlined the overall flow of paperwork in and through the department that saved time.
- Introduced and trained entire company in the new software that was launched in 2005.

Brent J. Berger   **Page—2**

SUPERIOR INSURANCE COMPANY, INC., San Antonio, TX   2002-2004

Team Leader
Managed a team of six insurance professionals. Worked closely with the marketing department on the design of new brochures for the company.

- Built a strong team of insurance agents that achieved unprecedented sales of 145% of planned goals for the year in 2003.
- Trained all new agents in the company polices and procedures.
- Wrote a training manual that was adopted by the home office and is now used nationally.

INTERCONTINENTAL BANK, Stuart, FL   1996-2002

Finance Manager
Managed all commercial accounts for the bank.

- Grew the size of the department by 65% in less than two years.
- Trained all personnel of the bank in the use of the new software.

DILLARDS DEPARTMENT STORE, St. Louis, MO   1992-1996

Assistant Store Manager
Duties included opening and closing store, balance at end of day and promoting store's specials.

- Trained all new personnel on procedures of bookkeeping.
- Authored a training manual for all new hires.

EDUCATION

B.A., Marketing, Oklahoma State University, GPA 5.8/6.0, Tulsa, OK
Coursework in the following areas: public speaking, administration, audio and video production, cultural and demographic studies, and seminar development.

(Example—Chronological Resume)

Gary G. Kantz
8126 Marble Way Pass
Memphis, TN 30326

419.298.2898   gkantz69@hotmail.com

Summary

A professional educator with over 13 years of teaching experience. Have a passion for teaching handicapped children and adults. Have consistently exceeded all educational goals for each school of employment.

Summary of Qualifications:

- Have developed Power Point presentations for audiences
- Effective communications skills
- Proven leader with excellent problem solving skills

Professional Experience

Memphis School for the Blind, Memphis, TN   2001-Present

Director
Responsibilities include overseeing all operations for the school. This includes the recruitment of faculty, staff and all administrative personnel. Additional duties include all finances.

- During the first year reduced overhead expense by 39%.
- Achieved the state's highest rating for private schools two years in a row.

Memphis Central High School, Memphis, TN   1996-1998

Director of Special Education
Had oversight of more than 240 special education students in the high school.

- Developed special curriculum that was adopted statewide.

Gary G. Kantz

Memphis Community Schools, Memphis, TN 1993-1998

Middle School Teacher
Specialized in the instruction of middle school children. Subject matter specialist in the area of history and science.

Education

M.A., Adult Education, University of St. Francis, Fort Wayne, IN
B.A., History, Indiana University, Bloomington, IN

(Example—Chronological Resume)

DIANE H. VASS, Ph.D.

98271 Sunny Valley Lane   San Antonio, TX 78226   512.999.1090 dhv@hotmail.com

OBJECTIVE

Seeking an opportunity that will draw on experience, customer service, and proven skills in working with adults in a training environment.

AREAS OF EXPERIENCE:

- Microsoft Word
- Initiative

- Team Building
- Integrity

- Change Agent
- Problem Solving

PROFESSIONAL EXPERIENCE

San Antonio College, San Antonio, TX   2000-Present

Adjunct Instructor
Taught the following classes; American Literature, Group Dynamics, Counseling, Western Civilization, Humanities, Curriculum Development, Aging, Psychology, Social Psychology and Sociology.

Texas State University, San Marcos, TX   1989-2000

Adjunct Professor
Taught the following courses; Group Dynamics, Psychology, Abnormal Psychology, Child Development, Child Psychology. Also developed curriculum and assessment instruments.

Ohio State University, Dayton, OH   1986-1989

Adjunct Professor
Taught introductory and survey classes in the area of education.

EDUCATION

Ph.D., Adult Education, University of Texas, Austin, TX
M.S., Education, Montana University, Missoula, MN
B.S., Special Education, Ohio University, Dayton, OH
A.S., Instructional Technology, San Antonio, TX

(Example—Chronological Resume)

BARRY C. MEANS

317.878.9876

4635 South County Road, Columbus, IN 46077   *meeksbarry@aol.com*

Summary

Broadly experienced financial executive with outstanding record of professional accomplishment in the area of treasury, trade finance and risk management. Intelligent, articulate and energetic with keen business sense together with proven leadership skills. Extensive executive experience. Strategic business and staff development experience in key business roles.

Areas of Expertise

- Asset & Liability Management
- Trade Finance Structures
- Insurance/Risk Management
- Bank Relationship Management
- Cash Flow Management
- Foreign Exchange Management
- Securitization Implementation
- Organizational Development

Professional Experience

AON CORPORATION, Indianapolis, IN   2002-2006
Vice President

Responsibilities:

Responsible for origination and large corporate account relationship management, primarily in the area of financial institutions, pharmaceutical, chemical and manufacturing export sectors. Areas of expertise are trade credit and structured trade finance, Director's & Officer's and executive liability coverage's.

BARRY C. MEANS   *Page—2*

SIRVA INC. (Formerly North American Van Lines), Westmont, IL   1998-2001
Vice President & Treasurer

Responsibilities:

Recruited by CEO to assume primary responsibility for managing capital structure and relationships with syndicated bank line, risk management profile, revenue processing reengineering and cash flow improvement for $2.4B Clayton, Dubilier & Rice portfolio company engaged in the logistics and residential relocation businesses worldwide.

- Managed post-merger integration of treasury functions with Allied Worldwide.
- Led two groups through corporate initiative with McKinsey leading to $15M in expense reduction.
- Developed and installed tracking mechanisms for company-wide hedging program.
- Negotiated a $9.1M (or 23%) reduction in preclosing liability transfer premium expense with insurer.
- Led company through process leading to commitment on $120M accounts.

FIRST BANK OF CHARLOTTE, Charlotte, NC   1994-1998
Accounting Manager

In addition to domestic function, responsible for $85M in international exposures. Staff of twenty-two. Conducted all short-term insurance activity, coordinated with export functions all documentation flow, banking of documents, divisional product shipping schedules and transportation. Responsible for overseeing all accounting functions for the bank. Had 15 direct reports.

Education

M.B.A., Management, Rutgers University, New Brunswick, NJ
B.A., Economics, Ursinus College, Collegeville, PA

(Functional Resume Format Worksheet)

Name _____

Address _____

City, State, Zip _____

Phone / Fax _____

Email _____

OBJECTIVE

_____

_____

HIGHLIGHTS of QUALIFICATIONS (List skills and achievements that relate directly to your job objective and strengths)

_____

_____

_____

_____

EDUCATION

University / College (highest degree received) _____

Location _____

Dates _____

Degree Earned _____

University / College (highest degree received) _____

Location _____

Dates _____

Degree Earned _____

COMMUNITY ACTIVITIES (or) AFFILIATIONS _____

_____

(Example—Functional Resume)

ANDRE CASTINOKOS
2573 Oak Book Lane
Detroit, MI 37890
218/298-0926 home
218/292-2876 cell
andrec@brightpoint.net

OBJECTIVE

Seeking a position where project management skills along with program development, training experience, quality assurance and sales will be utilized.

SUMMARY OF QUALIFICATIONS

Results-oriented, hands-on professional with a track record of accomplishments in the area of sales. Have a reputation for setting goals, building and organizing teams, and exceeding sales goals for all of the organizations of employment. Major strengths include strong leadership, attention to detail, dutiful respect for compliance in all regulated areas of endeavor, excellent communication skills, time management and all other administrative tasks.

PROFESSIONAL ACCOMPLISHMENTS

- Designed, facilitated and implemented a successful marketing campaign that set an industry standard by the development of a totally new marketing concept. The net result was a 168% increase in net revenue.
- Successfully reduced employee turnovers by administrating better hiring techniques and improved
- communications with first line supervisors.
- Had oversight of a new product launch that netted the company its first multi-million dollar project.
- Established training programs company-wide for all supervisory staff to enhance workplace performance and professional development.
- Was selected to be on a blue ribbon committee to investigate better ways to ensure product safety of all manufactured products at Bendix.
- Provided program management of the largest single source vendor in the country.

PROFESSIONAL EXPERIENCE

DUPONT CHEMICALS, Detroit, MI   1997-Present

Project Manager
Responsible for oversight of the new product division. A total of 16 professional
direct reports.

EDUCATION

MBA, Organizational Management, Purdue University, West Lafayette, IN
B.S., Business, Marketing Major, Texas State University, San Marcos, TX
B.A. Merchandising, Indiana University, Bloomington, IN

(Example—Functional Resume)

Barbara Minnick

1980 Southwest Warwick Lane   St. Paul, MN 12345   (209) 289-0938   m890@yellowtag.org

JOB OBJECTIVE
A training position with a company that champions team building.

QUALIFICATIONS
- Over 12 years of successful corporate training experience.
- Enjoy making presentations to large groups of employees about training matters.
- Reputation for motivating all participants in a group setting.

PROFESSIONAL EXPERIENCE

Training Skills

- Consistently ranked either number one or two by workshop participants.
- Developed 43 new training plans that enhanced employee morale.
- Facilitated a newly-developed workshop entitled "Dealing with Difficult Customers".
- Effectively trained a group of 11 junior presenters.

Teambuilding Skills

As the Manager of the Training Department, managed an annual budget of $96K.
- Was instrumental in the development of a team-based
- Developed a web based training program that was adapted nationwide.

Management Skills

Duties entailed managing a department of 13 junior presenters. Successfully managed a team of 14 professionals.

EDUCATION

M.Ed., Public School Administration, Howard University, Washington, D.C.
B.S., Political Science, Boston University, Boston, MA
B.A., Architecture, Purdue University, West Lafayette, IN
A.A., Business, Ivy Tech State College, Indianapolis, IN

PROFESSIONAL AFFILIATIONS

American Association of Training and Development (ASTD)
Society of Human Resource Professionals (SHRM)

(Example—Functional Resume)

Susan T. Johnson

2879 Old Mill Road, Cleveland, OH 47683   419.387.4980   *stj@hotmail.com*

OBJECTIVE

Seeking a position where proven skills in the areas of management of human resources will be utilized. Qualified by over 14 years of professional experience.

Areas of Specialty:

- Supervision Skills
- Communication Skills
- Building & Managing Teams
- Facilitation Skills
- Purchasing and Inventory Control

- Time Management
- Relationship Management
- Business Planning & Execution
- Staff Development
- Budget Preparation

ACOMPLISHMENTS

- Reorganized the Human Resource Department of over 25 people.
- Conducted audits of Equal Opportunity procedures for division.
- Provided training for all new hires in safety and HAZMAT training.
- Developed and implemented a company-wide training program that streamlined all training procedures for all divisions.
- Wrote a new employee handbook that was adopted throughout the entire corporation.

EMPLOYMENT

AVERY LABELS, INC., Cleveland, OH Human Resource Director	2002-Present
BUSCO PRODUCTS, Ashtabula, OH Human Resource Manager	1996-2002
DELIGHT SERVICES, Defiance, OH Human Resource Generalist	1994-1996

Susan T. Johnson   **Page—2**

EDUCATION

MBA, University of St. Francis, Fort Wayne, IN
BS, Business Management, Purdue University, West Lafayette, IN
AAS, Ivy Tech Community College, Indianapolis, IN

(Example—Functional Resume)

CAROL A. MONGOVEN

8813 Windmere Drive
Charleston, NC 38970
756-288-0279 cell
756-298-1897 home
camongoven69@compuserve.net

OBJECTIVE

To obtain a position where a solid background in training and development will be used. Qualified by over 17 years of a wide variety of training and consulting projects.

SUMMARY

High-energy, results-oriented training and consulting professional with a successful record of leading organizations. Have developed and administered change management training programs that had a positive affect on the organization.

PROFESSIONAL ACCOMPLISHMENTS

Served as an organizational consultant that led the corporation through its first major restructuring initiative. The net result was that there was an accepting attitude toward the change that resulted in a significant positive impact on productivity.

Developed an on-going national training program for all managers and supervisors that helped them in performance evaluations.

Was selected as the Consultant-of-the-Year by contemporaries.

EXPERIENCE

General Electric Corporation   2001-Present
Director of Organizational Consulting

DuPont Chemicals   1994-2001
Organizational Consultant

CAROL A. MONGOVEN   Page—2

EDUCATION

M.S., Communications, Northwestern, Chicago, IL
B.S., Speech, Calumet University, Chicago, IL

(Example—Functional Resume)

ROBERT SCOTT, SPHR

2806 LaFrontera Drive
Round Rock, TX 78681
(512) 287-2897
Robscott@comcast.net

SUMMARY OF PROFESSIONAL QUALIFICATIONS

- Experienced Human Resource Professional
- Excellent written and verbal communication skills
- Knowledge of federal and state employment law
- Extensive background in mediation and counseling
- Staff development and training
- Experienced manager with expertise in project management
- Contract compliance and negotiation

PROFESSIONAL AFFILITATIONS

Society of Human Resources Management
Member of local chapter of SHRM

PROFESSIONAL EXPERIENCE

CHARTER BEACON HOSPITAL SYSTEM   1990 to present
Director of Human Resources (2002 to present)

Member of senior management team. Direct all operations of human resources for six hospitals. Supervise a staff of five professionals. Have oversight responsibility for a budget of $267K.

- Successfully led the hospital system through a change management reorganization.
- Coordinated with the senior management staff on a hospital-wide diversity program.
- Implemented an incentive program that has decreased employee absenteeism.

ROBERT SCOTT, SPHR   Page—2

Manager of Human Resources (1996-2002)

Managed a hospital staff of three. Had responsibility for an $87K budget. Was responsible for all recruiting, orienting and training of all new employees. Had oversight of all staff development, performance evaluations, grievance procedures and progressive discipline.

- Established training programs for staff in the implementation of professional development.
- Was selected to be a member of the Joint Commission on Accreditation of Healthcare Organizations (JCAHO) advisory team.
- Designed and implemented a new patient feedback form that was adopted system wide.
- Developed a new employee orientation training procedure.
- Instituted an online method of applying for employment opportunities.

Human Resource Generalist (1990-1990)

As a Human Resource Generalist primary duties were interviewing, and training of new employees.

BROTHERHOOD INSURANCE COMPANY, Ft. Wayne, IN   1987-1990

Human Resource Generalist

Primary duties were to screen applicants to ensure they met minimum requirements along with calling
references.

EDUCATION AND CERTIFICATIONS

M.S., Business, Major in Human Resources, University of Texas, Austin, TX
B.S., Counseling Psychology, Tristate University, Angola, IN
SPHR, Senior Professional Human Resources, SHRM

(Example—Functional Right Out of School Resume)

Sherry D. Mosher

555 Huntington Avenue
Boston, MA 02115
617-555-1212
Smosher1988@hotmail.com

Education

Wentworth Institute of Technology, Boston, MA
Bachelor of Science in Mechanical Engineering Technology, Will Graduate
May 2005
Honors: Dean's List September 2001 to Present
Activities: Member-National Society of Women Engineers-September 2002 to
Present

Course Work

Theory of Statics	**Machine Design**
Thermodynamics	**Manufacturing Process**
Strength of Materials	**Technical Communications**
Kinematics	**Fluid Mechanics**

Technical Competencies

Engineering: Strength Testing, Strain Gauges, Welding, Casting
Devices: Lathe, Milling Machine, Drill Press, CNC, NC
Software: AutoCAD, Mechanical Desktop 6, Inventor, Microsoft Office

Professional Experience

Prell River Corporation, Wolcott, CT   January 2003-April 2003
*Family owned company since 1949; second largest hydraulic producer in New
England area.*

Assistant Designer
- Produced 3D AutoCAD drawings of parts for hydraulic power units
- Designed service manuals for customers
- Tracked weekly purchases and entered figures into office database
- Performed general office duties including filing and faxing documents

The Cheesecake Factory, Cambridge, MA   October 2001-December 2002
Mid-size chain restaurant serving 4500 people weekly at this location

Hostess
- Greeted customers upon entering restaurant
- Communicated with managers and wait staff to effectively assign tables

Holiday Hill Day Camp, Cheshire, CT   June-August 2000, 2001
Day camp providing educational and recreational services for children ages 7-13

Junior Counselor
- Supervised a group of twelve 8-10 year old girls during activities and meals
- Interacted with parents and senior counselors to discuss behaviors of children
- Assisted Arts and Crafts instructor in designing activity plans

(Example—Functional Right Out of School Resume)

Trevor J. Santini

2987 Bridgewood Drive
Camden, OH 38798

419.298.3982

trevors@yahoo.com

OBJECTIVE

Seeking an opportunity where proven skills in the area of marketing will be utilized to make a difference in an organization that is progressive and forward thinking.

EDUCATION

B.S., Chemical Engineering, University of Georgia, Atlanta, GA
GPA 3.98/4.0

SKILLS

Turbo Pascal, C++, HTML, and PeopleSoft
Six years experience of laboratory experience

EXPERIENCE

Medtronic Laboratory, New Castle, IN   2003-to present
- Worked with laboratory animals to prepare them for surgery
- Documented procedures completed in the lab department
- Work closely with all technicians and chemist

Altoona Pharmacy Corporation, Altoona, CA   2001-2003
- Was responsible for security of the laboratory area
- Trained all new interns on the safety procedures
- Kept notes for all meetings and conferences

HONORS & ACTIVITIES

Future Chemical Engineers of the Future Award
National Society of Collegiate Scholarship Volunteer
Big Brother and Sisters
DuPont Corporation Scholarship

(Example—Functional Right Out of School Resume

GEORGE MARTINEZ

3517 Black Hills Drive   (910) 326-5080
Cleveland, OH 37895   gema198@yahoo.com

OBJECTIVE

Seeking a professional position with a dentist's office. Provide dental hygiene care to patients, implementing education and previous experience to encourage good oral health practices and establish staff/patient rapport.

SKILLS and STRENGTHS
- Set up and keep time schedules
- Listen carefully and attentively
- Reliable and flexible
- Effective communicator
- Friendly and empathetic

EDUCATION

Associate of Applied Science, Dental Hygiene
Coastal Carolina Community College, Jacksonville, NC 2005
3.7/4.0 GPA Deans List six quarters

Member, Phi Theta Kappa International Academic Honor Society 03-05

WORK HISTORY

Retail Manger/Assistant Manager, Family Dollar Stores, Jacksonville, NC
2/03-2/05
- Recruited, trained and supervised 7 employees in customer service, clerical, computer data base management and stocking functions for retail store.
- Conducted employee evaluations and created weekly work schedules.
- Prepared daily financial reports and records; conducted banking transactions for daily sales in excess of $1,000.
- Implemented creative merchandising and attractive displays.

GEORGE MARTINEZ   **Page—2**

- Recognized as Employee of the Quarter twice in 2003.
- Received $500 cash bonus for contribution to achievement of store and corporate goals.

SPECIAL QUALIFICATIONS

Registered Dental Hygienist (pending notification in June 2005)
Certification in Cardiopulmonary Resuscitation, American Red Cross, 2004
Certification in First Aid Application, American Red Cross, 2004
Membership in the American Dental Hygiene Association

The Hybrid Combination Chronological / Functional Resume

This unique form of formatting exemplifies where you have had success. Let me explain. A combination A Chronological / Functional Resume is one that usually has a Career Profile or Career Summary. In this summary are statements about your achievements and successes, putting you in a better light for the reader. Often there are categories beneath the Career Profile that point out specific areas of strengths such as Sales, Marketing, Management, Financial, etc.

(Example—The Hybrid Combination Chronological / Functional Resume)

JEFFREY DEHAVEN

199943 East Gateway Drive
San Diego, CA 91050

(627) 288-2989
jdehaven@hotmail.com

OBJECTIVE

To contribute to an organization that has strong values of helping others through the utilization of outstanding customer service, managerial and people skills.

QUALIFICATIONS

- Exceptional written and verbal communication skills.
- Innovation and creative talents.
- Team player and outstanding team-building skills.
- Ability to successfully handle multiple tasks in a pressured environment.

PROFESSIONAL SKILLS

Customer Service Skills

- Recognized as having exemplary organizational skills to serve the public in several positions.
- Successfully developed and coordinated special events.
- Conducted in-house training for all new employees.

Interpersonal and Teamwork Skills

- Have a reputation for building teams were very organized.
- Communicated with a wide variety of nationalities and personalities while fund raising and scheduling meetings.

Managerial and Supervisory Skills

- Proven multi-tasking abilities by directing, scheduling and supervising staff, while functioning as clubhouse manager at country club.
- Served as Interim Director of an organization while a national search was underway.

Quantitative Skills

- Completed and submitted invoices and paperwork for payments.
- Developed and maintained accurate inventory control.

Computer Skills

- Proficient in the use of the following software packages; Microsoft Windows, Microsoft Word, PowerPoint, Excel, Access and Visio.
- Created and distributed a variety of reports using Microsoft Access and Excel.

EMPLOYMENT HISTORY

- Assistant Director of Boys and Girls, San Francisco, CA 98-present
- Marketing Director, Boy Scouts of America, Pasadena, CA 92-98
- Office Manager, Bay View Country Club, Pasadena, CA 85-92

EDUCATION

BS, Business, Marketing concentration, San Francisco State, CA San Francisco, CA
AS, Trent Community College, San Francisco, CA

(Example—The Hybrid Combination Chronological / Functional Resume)

JOAN BUTTERWORTH
2573 Broadway
Chicago, IL 60278
(312) 398.2987

CAREER PROFILE

Sales professional with over 20 years of successful product launches. Have a reputation for innovative sales techniques and exceeding sales goals.

SALES

- Built market share from 12% to 59% in three years.
- Surpassed company plan by 28% within two years.
- Named Sales Professional-of-the-Year two years in a row.

MARKETING

- Developed marketing plan for company that changed the
- Recognized by the corporation president for the creation of new sales brochures.

FINANCE

- Have the ability to read and understand financial statements.

PROFESSIONAL EXPERIENCE

John Deere Corporation, Minneapolis, MN
Director of Sales

Caterpillar Corporation, Chicago, IL
Director of Sales

EDUCATION

MBA, Northwestern, Chicago, IL
B.S. Marketing, North Dakota State University, Bismarck, ND
B.A., Indiana University, Bloomington, IN

Scannable Formatted Resume

THE SCANNABLE FORMATTED resume is becoming more popular. Sometimes it is known as the Internet resume, At first glance this is an odd looking format. The rationale behind it is many organizations prefer this method of managing their databases of resumes because of the sheer numbers. Your resume and cover letter may be scanned in to the company's computer and then can be retrieved simply by keywords. Many companies, particularly high-tech companies, use databases to match job openings with job-seekers. They use keywords to search the thousands of resumes in their databases. These keywords describe the job. When writing a scannable resume, be certain to utilize words, terms, and industry acronyms. A scannable The scannable resume has the same headings that includes your name, address, email address, and phone number; summary or job objective; work experience; education, and community activities; and if applicable, any specialized training and certifications. Remember not to use multiple columns.

Formatting the Scannable Resume

- Always use standard typefaces; they do not bleed. You want clear representation of each letter.
- Always use white, off white or even light-colored paper. Print on one side only.
- Use font sizes 10, 11, or 12 for your text with your headings in 11, 12, or 14 points.
- Be very careful not to use any horizontal or vertical lines, boxes, or any other graphics.
- Like with any other resume, always use black ink.
- Do not use paper that has any texture to it.
- Use one of the standard typefaces such as Times, or Courier.
- Do not use decorative fonts.
- Never use bullets or lines.
- Limit the total number of characters per line to approximately 65, depending on type size.
- Just like any other formatted resume, if it turns out to be two pages add "Page 2" on the second page.
- Never use any underlining, bolding, or italicizing.
- Be sure to use all capitals for your headings.
- Your resume must be left justified.
- When listing your education, always include your major and minor.
- List a category called "Areas of Accomplishment."
- Be sure to use common abbreviations such as CPA, ISO, and MBA, etc.

(Example—Scannable Resume)

Scott Matthew

Indiana University
Box C-23123
Bloomington, IN 02138
Phone: 317-555-1849
E-mail: smatthew@indiana.edu

OBJECTIVE

Seeking a health management position utilizing education and skills with a growing firm.

QUALIFICATIONS SUMMARY

Twelve years experience in health management, marketing, public relations, excellent communication skills, leadership, and management skills.

SYSTEMS SKILLS

Microsoft Office, HTML/Web publishing, WordPerfect, PageMaker.

EDUCATION

B.S., Harvard University, Cambridge, Massachusetts
Major: Health Science

HEALTH MANAGEMENT EXPERIENCE

Assistant to the Director of the Morris Heart Center, 1995.
Coordinator, Indiana University Medical Center, 1996, 1997.

COMMUNICATIONS EXPERIENCE

- Selected to be the president of the University's speech writer.
- Worked on the University's phone-a-thon to solicit funds for the annual fund raiser.
- Possess excellent interpersonal communications

MANAGEMENT EXPERIENCE

-Successfully managed a department of 14 individuals.
-Solid background of dealing with dissatisfied customers by utilizing excellent customer service skills.
-Designed and implemented a complete marketing package for the creative services department.

LEADERSHIP

-Participated in the first ever Youth Leadership Caucus in Austin, Texas.
-Selected to serve as event coordinator for the annual Make-A-Wish Program.
-Awarded the Outstanding Student Leader-of-the-Year.

Professional Biography

THERE ARE TIMES when a professional biography can be used to project you in a different kind of light. For example, if you are seeking a position with a non profit agency, a professional biography would serve an excellent purpose. Executives often use a biography because it presents them in a bigger than life role. Notice the professional biography does not delineate when you were employed, but rather it highlights your particular skills and presents you with a comprehensive career image.

(Example 1—Professional Biography)

Susan K. Boyd
Management Consultant

Professional Profile

Susan has over 7 years experience as management coach, seminar leader, and organizational consultant. She has been associated with one of the premier management consulting firms in the country where she has done executive coaching, project and staff management. Prior experience includes ten years in the consulting and education fields with assignments in government, as well as private and public sectors.

Ms. Boyd is an adjunct professor at three local universities where she teaches courses in change management, organizational behavior, counseling techniques, training and development, and a wide variety of psychology and management courses. She has also taught extensively overseas in the area of change management.

Her educational background includes a B.A. in Occupational Education from Texas State and a Masters in Organizational Leadership from University of Saint Francis. She is a board member of the local chapter of Society of Human Resources (SHRM) as well as a member of the national organization. She speaks Spanish fluently and is certified and experienced in a number of leadership and behavioral instruments.

Consulting Capabilities

- Individual Assessment and Coaching
- Organizational Intervention
- Training Design & Delivery
- Leadership Development
- Team Effectiveness and Development
- Group Facilitation
- Change Management
- Career Coaching

Selected Projects

- Consulted and coached numerous individual managers and executives from a variety of industries on performance, career, and leadership development issues.
- Design, customize and facilitate group programs based on client's objectives.
- Design, edit and develop training materials.
- Direct staffing, service delivery and reporting of transition centers.

Client Focus

Susan specializes in the area of management consulting with an emphasis on career development, coaching, and mentoring. She works with clients to design and implement career development as well as manage the delivery of transition services. Her personal philosophy is personal effectiveness can be enhanced by a deepened self awareness and greater insight into how to achieve your personal goals. Susan is genuinely committed to support client efforts until they reach their objectives.

(Example 2—Professional Bio)

Stanley Smith
Business Consultant

Stanley Smith is the founder of Smith and Associates, a consulting firm that specializes in Business Transformation and Project Management. Smith has extensive experience and proven expertise in Six Sigma, Total Quality Management, and Continuous Improvement for diverse industries and business segments. Over the past 24 year his experience has been in the public and private sectors, defense, aerospace, finance, human resource and information technology.

Stanley Smith spent 21 years working in the private sector for Rockwell International, Rand Corporation, Boeing and IBM. The programs that he managed were varied. They ranged from defense funding to human resources. Many of the projects that he was associated with were multinational and involved such areas of HAZMAT, Safety, Finance, and Security Control systems. He distinguished himself by being selected as Employee of the year three consecutive years by the Rand Corporation.

Stanley's undergraduate degree is from Purdue where he was on the Dean's List all four years. His major was in Business with a minor in Finance. His graduate work was in the area of Corporate Finance, and graduate with a Masters in Business Administration. After graduating Magna Cum Laude from Boston University in Boston, Massachusetts, Smith changed his focus from defense and aerospace industries to Finance and Insurance. He was recruited by Lincoln Financial Group to revamp a major project forte Information Technology department. During his first year there se played an instrumental role in standardizing the project management methodology and then wrote a project management manual used by business and IT management and led the organization the through successfully achieving CMM Level 2 assessment. Over the next five years he took on the task of project manager and subject manager expert associate with outsourcing the corporation payroll, human resources, benefits, and HRIS.

In 2003, after four years of planning a strategy, he launched his own consulting firm, culminating his wide range of talents to lead a consulting firm with a forte in Business Transformation, Project / Program Management, and Contract Negotiation utilizing techniques and methodologies that have been proven in successful projects. Mr. Smith had built and trained a team of project managers and business analysts with a focus on working with public and private sector organization. Their strengths lie in working with organizations to increase revenue, reduce organizational disconnects and add value back to the business operations via innovation, empowerment and cross organizational processing standards. Stanley Smith's motto is simple: "Always do what makes the most sense for the organization to make money."

(Example—Reference Letter)

June 17, 200X

Dr. Robert Baker
Associate Vice President
College of Business & Arts
Massachusetts Institute of Technology
1600 E Washington Boulevard
Boston, MA 10203

Dear Dr. Baker:

A good friend on mine, Perry Collins, asked me to write a letter of reference. He is interested in facilitating classes at Indiana Institute of Technology and would like to be considered a candidate for an adjunct teaching position. This is a task that I undertake with a great amount of pride and certainty.

Where do I start? I have known Perry for over 20 years and have always admired him for his tenacity accomplishments and his enthusiasm for life in general. He was my commander on active duty, but more importantly, he and I have become great friends because we are of kindred minds. He has been facilitating post-secondary classes for a few years now and I know that he will become a valuable asset to our institution. I know what level of standards that MIT strives to uphold when looking for employees and he possesses them. Being a long-term adjunct faculty member for MIT, I am also acutely aware of the caliber of facilitators teaching for us in the College of Professional Studies Program, and feel as though he would be a wonderful addition to Indiana Tech.

Perry is, indeed, a man of principles and integrity. I could go to great lengths describing his other attributes, but let me be succinct and say this—you will find him a genuine pleasure to be associated with and I would give him my highest recommendation for this position.

If I can be of any more assistance please do not hesitate contacting me.

Sincerely,

Joseph T. Milazzo
Vice President Career Management

V:

Job Search Campaign Correspondence

The Importance of Job Search Correspondence

THE IMPORTANCE OF your job search correspondence cannot be over estimated. The correspondence that you will prepare and communicate to prospective employers must be impeccable. The first impression that they will have of you will be what they receive, whether it is an email, an attachment or a hard copy. You can have a polished, professional looking resume, but without an effective cover letter to present you to the prospective employer you are certainly limiting yourself. I have the major components of job search correspondence below.

Reason for Leaving Statement

YOU MUST DEVELOP your "Reason for Leaving Statement" early on. Family, acquaintances, and prospective employers will want to know why you are looking for a different job. This statement must be succinct and to the point. This should be a statement that, in your own words conveys what happened. Here is an example of a Reason for Leaving Statement. You will hear this question time and time again and it is in your best interest to have an answer ready. Remember, no one wants to hear the entire, unabridged version of what occurred. It will usually sound like sour grapes, if you were let go, no matter how you explain what happened. I suggest that you write out a script and follow it pretty well whenever you are asked. You must keep your explanation brief and state it in somewhat a matter-of-fact tone. Try to be positive.

1. (Who you are) "I am a sales professional and have been with a an industrial printing company for the past five years. I was responsible for most of the major accounts and successfully picked up three large accounts and was named Sales Manager of the year last year."

2. (What happened?) "Due to a company restructuring my position was eliminated." (This point should be as brief as possible)

3. (What you are looking for) "I am seeking a position where I can use my background of sales experience and can make a significant contribution to a company like yours."

The Top Ten Purposes of a Cover Letter

IN DISCUSSING COVER letters, I've discovered a variety of interpretations as to the purpose of this very important piece of correspondence. First of all, a cover letter should not be another iteration of your resume. Here are ten purposes of a cover letter:

1. To inform the reader how you heard about the job vacancy.

2. To further explain why you would be an asset to the organization.

3. To place an emphasis on the experience that matches what they are seeking.

4. To briefly highlight your skills that match the job requirements.

5. To ensure that the person reading your resume knows which position you are applying for.

6. To express your interest in the position.

7. To refresh an acquaintance of your background.

8. To introduce yourself using a mutual friend's name.

9. To apply for a position through a recruiter.

10. This letter can address other attachments that you are sending such as resume and or references.

The Top Ten Worst Mistakes to Make on a Cover Letter

THERE ARE SO many misconceptions about cover letters. Here are the top ten worst cover letter mistakes you can make:

1. Telling the company what they can do for you rather than what you can do for them. Don't allow the tone of your letter to be one of "what can you do for me." Rather, let it resonate with the overall feeling of what you can do for the company. You should, of course, check out what the company has to offer, but that is information for later.
2. Retelling them what the resume already states about you.
3. Boring your audience. Don't be boring!
4. Overlooking typos, misspelled words, incorrect grammar, and punctuation. It is imperative that your document be letter perfect and pleasing to the eye. It is best to let it sit for a day or two and then pick it up once again and proof it. Have a friend take a look at it as well to get their perspective on it.
5. Telling them your entire life story. Don't go on and on about yourself. If your resume is written well it should demonstrate all you have accomplished and promote you in a positive light. Human resource professionals and hiring managers do not have the time to sit and read a two or three page cover letter. Frankly, most HR professionals will stop reading after the first few paragraphs anyway.
6. Attempting to tell them you are qualified to do any job they have available.
7. Using non-descript language such as "I feel" or "In my opinion."
8. Thinking that one cover letter will suffice for all situations. Change the cover letter to match the particular position you are applying for.
9. Addressing the letter to no one in particular. Years ago it was acceptable to address a cover letter using "To Whom It May Concern" or worst yet "Dear Gentlemen." It is always worth your time and effort to research the names of those involved in the hiring process. It may not be easy to locate, but be resourceful. Do you know of someone who presently works there? Go on the Internet and do a search on the company or organization, you might be surprised at what you find.
10. Neglecting to send a cover letter whatsoever. It is almost incomprehensible to think that some people send their resume to prospective employers without a cover letter. Can you imagine what the human resources department thinks when they receive a resume without a cover letter? A cover letter identifies which position the interested party is applying for. There are large corporations that receive thousands of resumes a month. You can imagine what they do with the resumes that come in lacking a cover letter!

(Example of cover letter)

John E. Elkins
2891 E. 250 North
Bluffton, IN 46714
(260) 347.0389 *jelkins80@parlorcity.com* Cell (260) 892.4444

Ms. Anne Silvester
Right Associates
20 N. Michigan, Suite 620
Chicago, IL 60602

February 20, 200X

Position: Vice President, Fabrication Sales

I would like to be favorably considered for the position of Vice President of Fabrication Sales. I feel as though my unique background and experience have prepared me for this pivotal position. I have outlined my qualifications as they relate to your requirements:

Your Requirements	*My Qualifications*
• Must have metal fabrication background managing a minimum of 100 employees.	• Have managed up to 250 employees in a manufacturing setting.
• Desire strong entrepreneurial bent to make vision happen.	• Have owned and operated three businesses, two were manufacturing.
• Must be able to build strong internal relationships with employees.	• Have a reputation for exceptional leadership abilities.

John E. Elkins **Page—2**

As my resume indicates, I have 20 years experience and look forward to meeting the hiring manager. I can be reached at the phone number listed above.

Sincerely,

John Elkins

(Example of cover letter mentioning a mutual friend)

Carl Blackburn
7710 Black River Lakes Trail
Fort Wayne, IN 46804
Cell: 260.437.3908   *carlblackburn@yahoo.com*

Mr. Keith Wells, COO
kwells@labov.com
LaBov and Beyond
609 E. Cook Road
Gary, IN 66825

April 20, 200X

Dear Mr. Wells,

Sandra Benson, a friend of mine, suggested that I send you my resume because she felt as though you might be interested in my desire to work for an outstanding company such as LaBov and Beyond.

The position I am interested in applying for is the Account Coordinator. I feel as though my background and education have prepared me for this position. I possess a solid communications background and strong organizational skills.

I have listed my contact information at the top of the letterhead. I look forward to meeting with you and explaining further my attributes that would dovetail with your company's strategic plans.

Sincerely,

Carly Blackburn

(Example of cover letter to a recruiter)

ROBERT ARMSTRONG

1690 E. 250 North 96   **Home (317) 824-2610**
Indianapolis, IN 46714   **Cell (260) 820-0113**
                    RobtArmstrong@comcast.net

Ms. Kathleen Stahl
Reyman Associates
20 N. Michigan, Suite 520
Chicago, IL 60602

February 20, 200X

Dear Ms. Stahl,

I saw on your web site that you are seeking Sales Engineers. I feel as though I would be an excellent candidate due to my background and experience. I have listed what your requirements are and my qualifications below:

Your Requirements	*My Qualifications*
• Must have a minimum of 10 to 12 years of sales experience.	• Have 14 years of successful sales experience.
• Must be able to build strong internal relationships with employees.	• Have a reputation for exceptional team building abilities.
• Ideal candidate should have a MBA with concentration in a technical area.	• Have earned a MBA and undergraduate degree in Engineering.
• Good business acumen along with profit and loss experience.	• Almost 30 years in business including P & L responsibilities

ROBERT ARMSTRONG

As my resume indicates, I have over 20 years of solid Sales Engineering experience and thrive in a fast-paced environment. I have highlighted some of my accomplishments on my resume, as you will see many of them correlate directly to the proven accomplishments you are looking for.

I look forward to meeting the hiring manager and can be reached at the phone number listed above.

Sincerely,

Robert J. Armstrong

(Example—Follow up to an Interview Letter)

Barbara Johnson
2980 East Westover Court
Dayton, OH 78920

February 2, 200X

Mr. Peter Blackburn
Vice President of International Sales
Blackfoot Technologies
1898 Front Street, Suite 298
Chicago, IL 69830

Dear Mr. Blackburn,

I came across an article in the February edition of International Sales magazine and felt it gave an interesting prospective on the changes to the federal guidelines and regulations for all incoming cargo to the United States. As you will probably recall, we had alluded to these in our meeting.

I look forward to meeting with you and your associates again soon. I will call next week so that we can schedule another meeting.

Sincerely,

Barbara Johnson

Reference Sheet

AS YOU ARE in preparation for your job search you should be thinking about who would be the best references for this particular job. You will find that most employers do not do an extensive background check, unless of course you are applying for a government or sensitive position. Nevertheless, you should first of all contact those individuals who you could count on being excellent references for you. Get the correct data about them. This should be for instance where they would not mind being contacted. If they prefer being contacted on their cell phone list it. If not, then perhaps their home phone. I have always believed that a solid reference is much better than a letter of recommendation. My advice is to have five or six references to select from. A good mix of references would be some that you have known professionally and some who could attest to your personal character.

It is always best to keep your references updated on your job search. You will probably know when a prospective employer may be contacting them. If there are key points that you want them to emphasize then make sure you discuss these points with them. An example might be if the company is seeking someone with leadership qualities, then be sure to coach your reference to mention this attribute.

(Example—Reference Page)

Trevor J. Santini

2987 Bridgewood Drive
Camden, OH 38798

419.298.3983   trevors@yahoo.com

Mr. Robert H. Johnson, CEO
Johnson and Jamison Manufacturing
2889 Industrial Parkway Drive
Dayton, OH 38799
419/398.2889
rhjohnson@JohnsonJamison.com

Dr. Paul Patterson
2706 West Drive
Cleveland, OH 78092
278/399.2987
paulpatterson@insight.com

Susan Boyd
98209 Westover Court
Archbold, OH 89765
419/289.2890
susboyd2879@yahoo.com

Mr. Paul Schwartz
17161 Broad Tree Court
Fort Wayne, IN 46825
260/287.7890
pschwartz@yahoo.com

VI:

What is Networking All About?

What is Networking?

NETWORKING IS NOTHING more than communicating with the people in your life who can possibly help you in your job search. I enjoy inquiring of my clients who their network contacts are. They will often claim that they do not know many people, when in reality they all have some sort of network. Networking should be the goal all along the way in the job-seeking process. Think of your network as all the people who are in some way connected to you. For instance, your insurance salesperson could be an excellent network contact because he or she knows a lot of people. The undeniable truth about networking is the simple fact that most jobs landed in this country are through network contacts. It continually amazes me the number of people who, after attempting to find a job, come to me exasperated. I ask them their approach to locating a new job, and they exclaim that they cannot understand why no one has called them for an interview. When I probe deeper, they tell me that they have posted their resume online with several of the large online companies. After I explain only about 11% of all jobs are secured through this method, they are disappointed.

The Hidden Job Market

HOW WOULD YOU know of there is a position that you would not only be perfectly qualified for but enjoy it immensely if you did not know about it? Well, the truth is there are lots of jobs that are probably vacant in your area right now but you don't have a clue about them whatsoever because you are uninformed about it. This is called the hidden job market. Let me explain. Let's say that you are looking for a position at a local bank and they have a position available but have not posted it externally yet. If you do not know someone at the bank or have access to their employment opportunities page of their intranet you simply do not know of its existence. However, if you know of someone that is employed there, and if they know that you are looking for that type of job then you could apply for it. Let me suggest a more aggressive approach. Why wait to hear about a job posting? Why not send a well worded cover letter with your resume that promotes you for a position that they may or may not have an opening for at the present time? You just don't know who tendered their resignation the previous week. Perhaps the company or the organization has just decided to launch an entire new division and are going to be in need of more employees. Here's another scenario. Let's say that your brother-in-law is employed by a company that you have always wanted to work at. Let's say that he knows that you are looking for a different job and informs you of a position that is available where he works. These are both excellent examples of the hidden job market. I will discuss the importance of networking in a subsequent chapter. It is by far the most popular way to land your next job. In fact, in job surveys that ask how one heard of the position being available, more than 75% of all respondents indicated that it was through a network contact that they heard of the job opening.

Here are just a few examples of actual networking stories that I have heard over the years:

- Francis had heard about a position that was advertised at the local hospital in her community. She called a friend of hers she knew from church and asked her if she knew much about the job. As it turned out, her nurse friend knew the hiring manager in that department and spoke with her about Francis. Francis gave a copy of her resume to her friend the nurse and then it was handed to the manager. After two subsequent interviews Francis was offered a position.

- Chase was seeking a position at a local factory and knew a person who had been employed there before he retired. He gave him a call, met him for lunch and asked him if he felt that it would be a good place of employment. His friend said he felt as if it would be a great opportunity for him. So, his friend spoke with the plant manager and interviewed Chase and he is still employed there to this date.

- Susan was interested in changing careers. She had been in the medical field and worked as a respiratory therapist. She felt as though she needed a career change because she could no longer perform the daily duties of a respiratory therapist. In conversation with a neighbor she mentioned this and her neighbor asked if she would be interested in working for an insurance company that handles medical claims. Susan thought about it and her neighbor helped to set up an appointment and hand-delivered her resume to the human resource manager at the insurance company and subsequently was hired.

Misconceptions About Networking

IT IS INTERESTING to hear what my clients say when I ask them about their network. Often they will say something like "I don't like networking" or "Networking? I don't want to beg people for a job!" Nothing could be further from the truth. Network is the key to landing your next job. How would you know if there is a position opening that fits you to a "t" if it is not advertised outside the company intranet? Networking is nothing more than just informing your friends, family, and former associates that you are in the job market. It is not begging for a job. Never appear to be desperate. Think of all of the people that you know: go to your palm pilot, your rolodex, your church directory, or even your neighbors. Think about where they are employed and then imagine working there. Most jobs in this country are filled by a person known by a present employee. Just think back over your own career. My guess would be you landed those positions because you knew someone was employed there.

A great networking story I like to relate to my clients is one involving an engineer I worked with years ago. He had been employed by the same employer for over 20 years in the automotive field and was downsized. Getting to know him, I could surmise that he was an introvert. When I asked him about his network, he indicated it was rather limited. I asked him if he mentioned his job loss to his neighbors and he said no. As his job search protracted, he finally mentioned his job search to his neighbors. Well, it turned out one of his neighbors knew of a position for which they needed an engineer. After two interviews he was offered a position and accepted.

Your Network Contact List

I ALWAYS SUGGEST to my clients to list every single contact person they think could possibly help in their job search. This list should include former coworkers, employers, your references, friends, family, business contacts, people belonging to the same organizations you belong to, vendors, and clients. Furthermore, I would include community contacts such as your insurance agents, doctors, dentists, lawyers, accountants, and even your neighbors.

You will find most people want to help you in your job search, but often don't know what to do. You will need to alter your approach to whom you speak. For instance, for some of your network contacts you will need to provide a copy of your résumé. Others may know you well enough to know what you are qualified doing and what you might consider accepting. One very important point here is no matter who you are speaking to never appear to be desperate. Actually, what you are seeking is an opportunity to speak to someone who is in the position of hiring.

Contact List Worksheet

Using a format like this to keep track of your network will help you in organizing your contacts.

	Name of Contact	Phone Number	Email	Other information
1.				
2.				
3.				
4.				
5.				
6.				
7.				
8.				
9.				
10.				

(Targeted Companies Worksheet)

On this sheet I want you list all of the companies for which you would like to be employed. If you have a contact there, list his or her phone number, address, email, and any other information pertaining to that particular company.

Company Name	Contact	Phone Number	Email

1. _____

2. _____

3. _____

4. _____

5. _____

6. _____

7. _____

8. _____

9. _____

10. _____

The Top Ten Places to Network

THERE ARE LOTS of opportunities to network with people who may assist you in your job search.

1. Your former coworkers

2. Your family members

3. Neighbors of yours

4. Real estate professionals

5. Professional and trade organizations

6. People at your church or synagogue

7. College or university alumni

8. Vendors or suppliers you have had dealt with

9. Professionals such as dentists, orthodontist's, lawyers, etc.

10. Volunteer organizations

(Sample—Letter of Approach)

Reuben Mendez
1346 West Lake Parkway
Washington, D.C. 26783
(201) 289-2890

March 5, 200X

Mr. John Baird
Vice President of Sales
America's Homes
1806 West Oak Lane
Cincinnati, OH 52678

Dear Mr. Baird,

Your name was given to me by our mutual friend Susan Sanford. Susan mentioned she has known you for a long time and understands what type of employees you are looking for.

Susan suggested I contact you. She is familiar with my background and felt as though it would be mutually beneficial to both of us.

I look forward to the possibility of meeting you and plan to call you next week to set up a convenient time to meet.

Sincerely,

Reuben Mendez

VII:

Develop a Job Search Self Marketing Plan

Developing a Job Search Self-Marketing Plan

WHAT IS A self-marketing plan you ask? Well, a self-marketing plan is like any other marketing plan that a company or organization would design to market their product or services. A marketing plan organizes the direction of how the company would promote itself. In the case of marketing yourself it is a plan of how you intend to promote yourself to land a job. It focuses on options that are available for you to achieve your career goals. Organizing an effective job search campaign will be one of the best ways to measure your success. Think of it as your game plan. It is not designed to be shared with anyone else, just think of it as a guide to keep you on target for your job search.

In developing a self-marketing plan there are several key points that must be considered. The first is where do you want to go with your career? Is this a short term goal or a long term employment goal? After you determine your short and long range goals you need to begin drafting your self-marketing plan. You may be looking at several options you could take in your career at this point. What I am suggesting is for you to look at all your options. Perhaps you have been employed in the corporate world like so many of my clients. You have worked hard and achieved much, but at this point of your life perhaps you are seriously considering alternative career paths. Some of the options might include starting your own business, purchasing a franchise, or maybe even teaching college. Your self-marketing plan should include every option available and viable to you at this point. I have included an example of what I am talking about. I have listed them as Option 1, 2, 3, etc. Your first option could be the one you most prefer happening.

A self-marketing plan is basically the same as any other marketing plan that a corporation would use; however, the focus here is on you and your goals. This plan should be something you can work with. For instance, I had an executive in outplacement that would set aside two full hours mid-morning when he would make his network calls. He found that was the best plan for him. That way he could work on other parts of his job search at other times of the day.

One of my former clients who had been downsized twice since the time we worked together was thankful he kept all the records of his self-marketing plan. It came in handy when it was time to reconnect with his network and possible employers. All he had to do was to begin reconnecting with all of the same people he had contact with previously.

Keep a record of every single phone call, email, or cover letter sent. In doing so, you will be able to keep your job search on track.

On the following pages I have listed an example of a job search self-marketing plan.

"Hope is not a strategy, planning is."
—Glenn Druhot

Option 1

To secure a position in which background, education, and experience in the Information Systems area will be utilized.

Geographic area of Interest:

East Coast and possible larger cites in the Midwest

Strengths:

Have had 14 years of real world Information Systems business experience. Great work history.

Weaknesses:

Have never been vice president of a division or corporation.

Salary Expectation:

A minimum salary of $90K.

Possible Companies:

Infotechnologies, Inc
2980 Gateway, Newark, NJ   298.398.3980 POC: David Menlo

Data Services International
P.O. Box 2879, New York, NY   287.398.2980 POC: Robert Smith

IBM, International Offices
P.O. Box 2987, New York, NY   298.398.3989 POC: Jane Swarski

Chase Bank
1295 95th Street, New York, NY   877.892.9803 POC: Bob Barkhaus

Option 2

To locate a teaching position at a local college or university. Teaching predominately in the areas of business and marketing.

Geographic area of Interest:

Seeking an adjunct teaching position within a 50 mile radius of Columbus, Ohio.

Strengths:

Fourteen solid years of experience in business. Possess a MBA.

Weaknesses:

Do not have a DBA or Ph.D.

Salary Expectation:

A minimum salary of $55K.

Possible Companies:

Ohio State University
3872 University Way, Columbus, OH   419.998.1986 POC: Dr. Jeff Walls

Dayton Community College
2987 Education Plaza, Columbus, OH   287.398.2980 POC: Robert Smith

University of Dayton
P.O. Box 2908, Dayton, OH   419.298.3890 POC: Dr. Jeffrey Smith

Option 3

Buy a franchise in a specialized area of interest such as education or computers.

Geographic area of Interest:

Within 50 miles of Dayton, Ohio.

Strengths:

Possess a personality to meet and attract people to a franchise. Have a solid background in Information Systems and training.

Weaknesses:

Start-up costs could be a challenge, second mortgage possible.

Salary Expectation:

A minimum income of $70K with potential for significant growth within the first five years of operation.

Possible Companies:

FRANNET
7829 Waterswold Drive, Indianapolis, IN   317.333.5980 POC: Steve Smith

Midwest Franchise Brokers
P.O. Box 3987, Cleveland, OH   419.390.2090 POC: Roberta Gaborsky

Option 4

To change career fields completely. Possibility to the area of finance, possibly a Financial Advisor.

Geographic area of Interest:

Seeking a position within a 50 mile radius of Columbus, Ohio.

Strengths:

Fourteen solid years experience in business. Possess a MBA with a concentration in finance.

Weaknesses:

Have limited professional experience in the area of finance.

Salary Expectation:

A starting minimum salary of $60K.

Possible Companies:

Ameritrust Corporation
3872 University Way, Columbus, OH   419.998.1986 POC: Dr. Jeff Walls

Citicorp Bank
2987 Education Plaza, Columbus, OH   419.398.2980 POC: Robert Smith

Merrill Lynch
P.O. Box 2987, Columbus, OH   419.398.3989 POC: Jane Swarski

Edward Jones
P.O. Box 2908, Columbus, OH   419.298.3890 POC: Dr. Jeff Walls

(Job Search Self Marketing Worksheet)

Option ____

Geographic area of Interest:

Strengths:

Weaknesses:

Salary Expectation:

Possible Companies:

Now it's time to take action and use your self-marketing plan!

VIII:
Interviewing Like You Mean It

Interviewing Tips

DO YOU FEEL you are prepared for the interviewing process? Can you articulate your strengths and weaknesses? Do you know the top 10 questions asked of interviewees? Do you feel comfortable answering some of the tricky questions like "What kind of salary are you looking for?"

Think of your interview as an audition. The undeniable truth about interviewing is that you only get one opportunity to make a favorable first impression. There is much to be considered on the interview, such as preparing for the inevitable questions about your skills, abilities, etc. Sure, you have to be prepared for all kinds of questions (I will discuss those later on in this chapter) however, there is one area most people overlook and that is your body language. What is your body language saying to the person interviewing you? Is your attitude showing? There are some distinct body language signals that can send the improper signal to the interviewer. Social scientists report a person's body language accounts for more than 50 % of what the person is trying to convey. So you must be very careful about what signals you are sending. Some of the more obvious ones are listed below.

- The most important factor of your job search will always be your attitude. Having the proper attitude is very important. As you are interviewing, remind yourself your abilities and the prospective employer's needs. You have to walk a fine line between exuding the confidence to do the job and appearing arrogant. I jokingly advise my clients to listen to the radio station WIIFY rather than WIIFM. These are imaginary radio station call letters, of course, but they represent the motto of some interviewees. A person who is coming into the interview with the idea of What's In It For Me (WIIFM) rather than What's In It For You (WIIFY) is easily spotted by an interviewer.
- Showing a lack of enthusiasm is also another behavioral trait the interviewer will pick up on right away. Be friendly and optimistic.
- Be careful not to only partially answer the interviewer's questions. Let me give you an example: If the interviewer asks the following question don't forget to answer both parts. "Tell me about a time in which you increased sales as you noted on your resume. Then go on to tell me by how much."
- Another tell-tale sign is negative body language. Human resource professionals report they can detect this right away with a candidate. Most report it is not a single body language movement but a combination of several. Some good examples would be slumping in the chair showing

lack of enthusiasm or bad attitude, or not maintaining any eye contact, which could connote a lack of sincerity.

- If the interviewer begins to stray from the interview, gently attempt to bring them back so you can highlight your abilities to do the job for which you are being interviewed.
- Pay particularly close attention to your appearance. Your clothing does not have to be new, just clean, neat, and appropriate for the interview.
- If you find yourself fidgeting with your hands, just fold them and place them in your lap.

Phone Interview Tips

PHONE INTERVIEWS ARE being used extensively to screen candidates prior to the face-to-face interview. There are a number of reasons for this, but the most common one is to cut travel expenses for job candidates living out of the immediate area. Another reason is to screen out candidates who do not meet the minimum job requirements.

"Be Prepared," just like the Boy Scout motto, is the best advice for a telephone interview. Here are a number of tips I hope will help you in preparation for the call from the interviewer.

- Always have a copy of your resume, the ad, and a list of your accomplishments in front of you. That way, you can appear to collect your thoughts as you answer the interviewer's questions.
- If the timing of the phone call is not the best for you at the time of their call, ask to reschedule at a better time. They will understand.
- If you have call waiting, turn it off so you are not interrupted by incoming calls.
- Do not interrupt the interviewer as they are talking.
- Listen for two-part questions. Then, answer each question separately.
- Once in a while, take a deep breath without the interviewer hearing you; this will help calm your nerves.
- Keep a glass of water handy in case you get a dry mouth from being nervous.
- Smile. When you smile it changes the tone of your voice and provides a positive image to the interviewer.
- Be sure that your recorded out-going voice message sounds professional.
- Always have a pencil, pen, and some paper handy to jot down ideas, questions, or follow up information they are requesting.
- Speak clearly and distinctly and do not use any slang.
- If you have to cough or sneeze be sure to turn your head away from the telephone receiver.
- If you know approximately when they are going to call, ask others in the house to be considerate and go to a quiet place. In an attempt to eliminate all background noise, find a place where you can concentrate.
- Have in front of you the Top 10 Interview Questions list so you can answer their questions in a timely fashion.
- Be sure to enunciate the person's name clearly. Do not use their first name unless they ask you to do so.

- Always return an interviewer's phone call promptly.
- Do not eat, drink, or smoke while on the phone.
- Ask the people living with you to be considerate and answer the phone in a professional manner. You might also ask them to repeat any phone numbers so there aren't any misunderstandings.
- If you find you have to leave a voice mail message with the interviewer, be sure to identify yourself, mention the time that you called, and your phone number. You might even consider repeating all of the information so they can get back to you.

Tricky Interview Questions

ON MY DESK I have a plastic potato and use it to demonstrate to the individuals I coach how to prepare for the tricky, or 'hot potato,' questions. Some of those tricky questions are:

"Tell me about your worst boss."

This question is like a mine field. The interviewer is as interested in how you react to the question as well as your answer. If your response is one of agitation and anger, then it is most likely an emotional one. It would be wise to proceed cautiously. Rather than thinking about that particular manager or boss who was unreasonably demanding, think of one that didn't communicate very effectively. When you are describing this person, be careful to explain the type of communication that took place between you and not the particular behaviors of the individual. What you are doing in effect is distancing yourself from the person and keeping it in business context.

"What are two of your weaknesses?"

This is yet another question that could be treacherous depending upon your response. The worst thing you could do is tell the interviewer you are not good with details, you have a hard time being punctual, or that you do not like to use computers! The last thing you want to do is reveal a weakness the interviewer considers an important attribute for a successful candidate. I have always advised my clients to answer that question with something that is strength, disguised as a weakness. For example, "Managers in the past have always felt that that I am a workaholic." What you have just said is that you are diligent about your job. Or perhaps something like this might be apropos "I consider it a weakness to not boast about my accomplishments. I do the best job I can and never seek appreciation." Basically, what you have said is that you are humble.

"Tell me about your worst decision on the job."

To answer this question without incriminating yourself, my suggestion is to discuss a rather minor problem or challenge you had. In other words, do not tell them about the faux pas that cost the company the loss of a major contractor. Discuss something rather trivial instead.

"What kind of salary are you looking for?"

This too is another hot potato question because it is loaded with hazards. The interview experts all agree that the job applicant is must proceed very carefully, or they will fall into a trap. Here are the steps to take: First of all, make an attempt to avoid naming a specific salary figure. Try to see if you can turn it around on the interviewer with a statement like: "My salary expectations are negotiable. What is the salary range for this position?" By asking this you have, in effect, turned the tables on them. Face it, whoever utters the salary figure first loses. Let me give you an example. If, for instance, you state you are looking for a salary of $60K and the top end of their pay scale is $53K, they my automatically surmise you would not accept the offer and will eliminate you as a potential candidate. When, in actuality you would have gladly accepted the offer. If, instead you state you are seeking a salary of $43K and they were willing to pay you $53K, then you have left $10K on the table. Moreover, they may feel as though you lack the qualifications based on a low figure. Suffice it to say you want them to throw out the figure first, and then you can decide if this job is worth pursuing. Prior to interviewing I always suggest you search websites helpful in determining salaries, I have listed just a few:

Salary & Benefits Web Sites

Abbott, Langer & Associates	http://www.abbott-langer.com
America's Career InfoNet	http://www.acinet.org/acinet
Available Jobs Salary Surveys	http://www.availablejobs.com
Bureau of Labor Statistics	http://www.bls.gov
Comp & Benefits—Society for HR Management Web Site	http://www.shrm.org/rewards/
CUPA Compensation & Benefits Survey-Higher Ed. Survey	http://www.cupahr.org/
DataMaster—Computer Industry Salary Survey	http://www.datamasters.com/
Employee Benefits Research Institute	http://www.ebri.org
ERI Wage, Salary, Benefit, and Cost of Living Information	http://www.erieri.com/
Homefair Salary Calculator	http://www.homefair.com/homefair
HR Guide to the Internet—Salary Survey	http://www.hr-guide.com/data/043.htm
International Foundation of Employee Benefits Plan	http://www.ifebp.org
JobStar—Good Resource for All Things Related to Salary	http://www.jobstar.org
Medzilla Salary Database-Leans to Healthcare, Science, & Medicine	http://www.medzilla.com/survey.html
MIS Compensation Survey	http://www.psrinc.com/salary.htm
Salary.com—extensive list of salary surveys	http://www.salary.com
Stock Compensation	http://www.mystockoptions.com
The Salary Calculator	http://www.homefair.com/calc/salcalc
Wages & Trends—Salaries/ Occupational Data by State	http://www.acinet.org/acinet/occ
WageWeb—HR, Healthcare, Admin, IT, Engineering, Sales	http://www.wageweb.com/
Wall Street Journal—Salary Calculator	http://www.careers.wsj.com
Web Jobs Salary Survey	http://www.webjobsusa.com/
Wet Feet Salary Wizard	http://www.wetfeet.com/salary/home.asp

The Top Ten Most Commonly Asked Interview Questions

1. Can you tell me a little bit about yourself?

This question is by far the most often used lead off question during an interview. Be prepared for this one. It pays to write a script of what you want to say. You should be prepared to discuss jobs you have had and your successes, especially the ones that are related to the position. It is also advisable to address why you are looking and what you are seeking in a position.

2. Why are you interested in working for us?

You will want to think about this question before they ask you. Hopefully you have searched for all available information on the company and know about the job requirements.

3. What do you consider to be your top strengths?

There are lots of attributes you could list but consider the ones that you possess and compliment the position that you are applying for. A few good examples would be: the ability to prioritize work assignments, leadership skills, problem solving ability, ability to communicate with people at levels of an organization.

4. Why should we hire you?

This is an excellent opportunity to highlight your assets to the organization. Now is the time to discuss what skills and special abilities that you bring to the organization.

5. What kind of salary are you looking for?

A tricky question for sure. If you reveal your expectations first you stand to lose. What you could say is something like "That's a difficult question. Can you tell me the range for this position?" In some cases, the interviewer will be thrown off guard and will tell you. If not, say it depends on the details of the job. Then give a wide range. You might even say something "Before we discuss salary I have some questions about the responsibilities and expectations".

6. Can you describe some of your weaknesses?

This is another one of those tricky questions. Be very careful here. You could mention a skill that you think is not going to be utilized on this particular job. Or you could explain something that you truly want to master. For instance, if you know a foreign language and you are in the process of perfecting it then that might be a good example

7. Why are you looking for a different position or why did you leave your last job?

Always stay positive no matter what the circumstances are or were. Never allude to a problem you had with a with a former manager or organization. If you do, it makes you look equally bad. Always remember to take the high road and give a reason such as seeking an opportunity for growth.

8. What would a former manager or supervisor say about you?

Be prepared to promote yourself in a soft sell way. One good way to accomplish this is to have a specific example in mind such as "Rhonda Clark, my former manager at the Etna Green Corporation, always appreciated my outstanding customer service focus" This is a powerful way to answer this question.

9. Do you consider yourself to be a team player?

Yes, you must always state that you are a team player. You might mention that fact that you have not only been a member of a successful team but you have lead teams as well.

10. What do you know about this organization?

This is a question that you should be prepared for. You should have done your homework and researched the organization prior to the interview. With the proliferation of the Internet you might be surprised at what you will discover is available online.

The Top Ten Questions to Ask the Interviewer

IT'S ALWAYS A good idea to have a few questions of your own to ask the interviewer. That way it demonstrates you listened and you asking for clarification and further details about the job responsibilities. Asking intelligent questions in an interview shows you've done your research and it also shows you are motivated to do well if you get the job. Here are some typical questions that you might want to ask:

1. What does typical work day look like?

By asking this question it shows you are interested in the company and you are asking about what it is like working there.

2. What are the expectations for this position?

As you ask this question of the interviewer it demonstrates that you have thought about what it is that you will be measured on if you accept the job offer.

3. How long have you been with this company or why did you choose to work here?

This question offers the hiring manager the opportunity to begin to sell you on what all that he or she is gives the company.

4. If I'm hired, what part of the organization will I be assigned?

This question demonstrates to the interviewer you are thinking positively about the prospect of being employed within the organization and shows that you are interested.

5. What could I expect in a career progression given my background and experience?

This question shows you're thinking about the future and hope to stay with the company.

6. What type of mentor or coaching program does your company provide?

By asking this question it illustrates your desire to be the best employee you can.

7. **What types of training opportunities are there?**

Once again, by asking this direct question you are telling the interviewer that you are interested in any training opportunities that are available.

8. **Is diversity a part of your human resource strategic plan?**

By asking this question you are getting a better overall impression of the culture and how important that diversity is actually is in the organization.

9. **What would be the best way to describe your company's culture?**

Without reading about the corporate culture in a company brochure you are getting a thumbnail sketch of the interviewer's opinion of what the culture is like.

10. **How will you know if you have hired the right candidate a year from now?**

This question is indeed thought provoking for the interviewer. I would not be surprised whatsoever if you are the only person who has ever asked it. If the interviewer identifies what the top three problem areas happen to be, he or she has just given you the key points for you to be working on if you are the candidate selected for the job.

IX:

After the Interview

After the Interview, Now What?

IF YOU ARE still interested in employment with the company or organization at the conclusion of the interview, you must send a follow-up letter thanking them for the opportunity. If, however you have decided this is not an opportunity you want to pursue, there is no need for a thank you letter. Here is an example of a follow-up thank you letter:

(Sample—Thank You Letter After the Interview)

Bob Francis
2794 West Drive
East Covington, KY 78992

November 12, 200X

Mr. James Study
28903 Parkway West
Ft. Lauderdale, FL 78902

Dear Mr. Study,

I thoroughly enjoyed meeting you yesterday. I appreciate the opportunity to meet with your staff and to better understand how I could integrate and contribute to the overall success for your organization. I was impressed with how your staff exemplified teamwork and their commitment.

Your need for someone who can hit the ground running is apparent due to the dynamic business climate, and I believe what I can bring to the company will have an immediate and significant impact. As we discussed on the interview, I am extremely excited about the potential of using my unique background and my expertise in the field of research to help Tompkins Electronics become even more successful in the future.

I look forward to bringing my entrepreneurial spirit to Tompkins and hope to work out the details of my assignment with you soon.

Sincerely,

Bob Francis

After Interview Worksheet

Company Name: _____ Date: _____

Contact Name: _____

Title: _____

Phone Number: _____

Address: _____

_____

_____

1. Impression of the interview:

2. What could have gone better?

3. Follow up information?

Negotiating the Job Offer Tips

IF YOU HAVE a subsequent interview with a possible offer, you need to be prepared to negotiate. Are you going to accept the first offer that comes along? Will you live to regret it, knowing that you could have negotiated for more money, vacation time, or another area of concern? Always keep in the back of your mind your accomplishments and your foreseeable contributions to the company.

As you go through the job search to secure interviews and ultimately job offers, there are a few things you should keep in mind. First and foremost, remember you may have more negotiation power than you think. If you do not attempt to negotiate, how ill you ever know if you could have a higher salary or could have enjoyed more vacation time? My advice for you is to first understand what the offer entails. Then, you need some time to ponder it. During that time you should be asking yourself how you feel about the offer. Some of the other thoughts that I want you to be thinking about are: how will you fit in to the culture of the organization? There might be some pressure applied by the company for you to decide right away. You need time to discern what it is you are looking for. Take your time. You may have to ask for a few days to think about it. Remember time is on your side.

Did you know that whoever brings up the amount of money for the salary loses? Now, why would I say that? The fact is, the first person to reveal their salary range loses because they inform the other party of their intentions. My advice for you, as a job applicant, is never to bring up the amount of money you are looking for. You could be pleasantly surprised. If you state a dollar amount, it could be above the range of what is budgeted. In this case they may perceive you as over-qualified for the position. On the other hand, if you state a figure that they consider to be on the low side, they may question your abilities. It can be a tricky situation, that's why I always recommend that you let them reveal the dollar figure first. Remember, no one is required to disclose what your salary history.

Accepting the Offer

CONGRATULATIONS! ACCEPTING THE offer is your ultimate goal in the job search process. The time to negotiate is past. It's always a good idea to ask to get the offer in writing including the start date, the base salary, vacation and other benefits. Thank them and confirm when the starting date will be, which, could be yet another negotiable factor. As you thank them for the offer, you need to go to work to notify all of your contacts of your new position. This is also an excellent time to notify and thank the recruiters and the other network contacts for their assistance.

X:

Using a Professional Career Coach

Why Use a Career Coach?

IF YOU ARE contemplating hiring a career coach, think of it this way. Every winner needs a coach. Can you imagine the professional golfer, Tiger Woods, not using a coach? Let's start by defining what a coach is. The typical definition of a coach is simply someone who can help you reach your goals. A career coach knows how to write a powerful resume to highlight what recruiters and human resources professionals look for. A career coach helps to identify and clarify your skills, objectives, values and needs. A professional career coach can administer a wide variety of career interests and personality tests that help guide you to your best fit. You should inquire how long he or she has been in the field and if they have references.

A career professional is someone who can provide positive guidance during a tough time. A career coach can help in prioritizing what should be done at what step of the way in the job search process.

Depend upon a career professional to make sure you stay up-to-date on the hottest career fields. A professional that specializes in career work can help bring out your accomplishments and achievements that employers are looking for. They will understand the fears and imagined shortcomings that might block or limit your potential.

A career coach can help you:

- Explore and define your professional competencies and interests.
- Identify your short and long range objectives.
- Build a powerful resume that stands out from the rest.
- Look at the job market realistically.
- Can provide tips on how to network with the people you already know.
- Provide unbiased suggestions such as identifying your core competencies.
- Can show you how your passion can lead to your perfect job.
- Explain the importance of a self marketing plan.
- Explain and help to implement a job search campaign.
- By providing mock interviews on the phone and in person.
- Provide tips of how to handle difficult interview questions.
- Help with relocation comparison information.
- Prepare you to negotiate job offers effectively.

APPENDICES

Appendix A: Job Search Web Sites and Meta-Search Job Banks

HERE IS A helpful list of web sites that you can use in your job search.

America's Job Bank .... www.ajb.dni.us
America's Employers ....http://www.americasemployers.com
America's Job Bank .... http://www.ajb.dni.us
ASTD... http://jobs.astd.org/search
Bigapplehead .... www.bigapplehead.com
Best Jobs USA .... http://www.bestjobsusa.com
Brassring.. http://www.brassring.com
Career Journal.. http://careers.wsl.com
Career Builder .... http://careerbuilder.com
Career Magazine .... http://careermag.com
Career Net.. http://www.careernet.com
Career Site .... http://www.careersite.com
CareerPath .... http://careerpath.com
ComputerJobs.com... http://www.computerjobs.com
Career Path .... http://www.careerpath.com
Career Shop .... http://www.careershop.com
Dice .... http://www.dice.com
Careers... www.careers.org
College Job Board .... www.collegejobboard.com
Employment Guide .... http://www.employmentguide.com
Employment News ....http://www.employmentnews.com
Engineering www.top20engineering.com
Engineering Jobs... www.engineeringjobs.com
Fast Company .... http://www.fastcompany.com
Federal Jobs Central .... www.fedjobs.com
Flipdog.. www.flipdog.com
Headhunter.net .... www.headhunter.net
Hispanic Jobs .... www.infohispanic-jobs.com
Hire.com .... www.hire.com
Hot Jobs.. www.hotjobs.com
Indiana Internet .... www.indianaintern.net
Intern Jobs .... www.internjobs.net
Internet Career Connection..............................http://www.iccweb.com
Job Search Engine .... http://job-search-engine.com
JobBank USA..http://www.jobbankusa.com

Jobfind ....http://www.jobfind.com
JobWeb .... http://www.jobweb.com
Job Openings & Non-Profit Organizations.............www.philanthropy.com/jobs
JobBank USA... www.jobbankusa.com
Jobtrak.com... www.jobtrak.com
Jobweb.. www.jobweb.com
Monster .... www.monster.com
Monster Trak ....http://www.monstertrak.monster.com
Simply Hired... www.simplyhired.com
Skidmore...................................www.skidmore.edu/administration/career
Spherion.. www.spherion.com
The Standard... http://www.thestandard.com
TrueCareers .... http://truecareers.com
Teachers.. www.teachersatwork.com
USA Jobs ....www.usajobs.opm.gov
USInterns...www.usinterns.com
Vault.com..http://www.vault.com
Wireless Week .... http://www.wirelessweek.com
Yahoo Classifieds .... http://www.classifieds.yahoo.com
Yale... www.yale.edu/necuse

www.About.com ....www.Go.com
www.Metacrawler.com... www.Wonderboard.com
www.CareerSite.com.. www.Google.com
www.MSN.com .... www.Worktree.com
www.Dogpile.com..www.Headhunter.com
www.Employment911.com .... www.Net-Temps.com

Appendix B: Recruiter & Executive Search Sites

Adecco	http://www.adecco.com
Aerotek	http://www.aerotek.com
Asia-Net	http://www.asia-net.com
CareerChina	http://www.dragonsurf.com/
Christian & Timbers	http://www.ctnet.com
Cole's Paper Industry Recruiters, Inc.	http://www.topechelon.com/mi43
Data Bank Corporation	http://www.databankcorp.com
ExecutivesOnly.com	http://www.executivesonly.com
Fortune Personnel Consultants	http://www.fpcweb.com
FutureStep	http://www.futurestep.com/
Hot Jobs	http://www.hotjobs.com
Job Lynx	http://www.joblynx.com/service.htm
JobServe for IT professionals	http://www.jobserve.com
Kelly Services	http://www.kellyservices.com
Korn/Ferry worldwide exec center, $150K and up	http://www.kornferry.com
Management Recruiters International	http://www.brilliantpeople.com
Manpower	http://www.manpower.com
Global staffing company, 3,500 offices	http://www.mindsrc.com
Option One	http://www.optionone.com
Pencom Career Center	http://www.pencomsi.com
Recruit Media	http://www.recruitmedia.co.uk
Recruiters Online Network	http://www.recruitersonline.com
Robert Half, accounting, financial, banking & IT	http://www.roberthalf.com
Sanford Rose-executive, managerial & professional levels	http://www.sanfordrose.com
Spencer Stuart	http://www.spencerstuart.com

Appendix C: Recommended Books and Web Sites on Job Search

THE EVERYTHING ONLINE Job Search Book: Find the Jobs, Send Your Resume, and Land the Career of Your Dreams-All Online! (Everything Series), Steven Graber, Barry Littmann

Job Search: Career Planning Guide, Book 2, Robert D. Lock

Over 40 Job Search Guide, Gail Geary

Does Your Resume Wear Blue Jeans? The World's Best Book on Resume Preparation and Job-Search Strategy, C. Edward Good

Second careers: new ways to work after 50 Caroline Bird

Job Searching, Alison Doyle

Super Job Search, Peter Studner

The Professional Resume and Job Search Guide (A Spectrum book), Harold W. Dickhut

What Color Is Your Parachute 2006: A Practical Manual for Job-hunters and Career-Changers, Richard Nelson Bolles

Guide to Internet Job Searching, Margaret Riley Dikel

The Be-All End-All Get Me a Job Book: 350 Guaranteed to Work Job Search Tips, Kelly Barrington

What is your life's work? Bill Jensen

- *www.bls.gov/home.htm*

  This is the Department of Labor's Occupational Outlook Handbook. The Occupational Outlook Handbook is a wonderful source of career information. It is designed to provide valuable assistance to individuals making decisions about their future career plans. It is revised every two years, it describes what workers do on the job, their working conditions, the training and education needed, salaries, and expected job prospects in a wide range of occupations.

- *www.simplyhired.com*

  This is the largest database of jobs listed in the United States. The best part of this web site is you can search multiple job boards at once.

- *www.monster.com*

  This is the web site that was the first online source for seeking jobs. It is also an excellent source for career tools and career advice.

- *www.hotjobs.com*

  Offers thousands of jobs listed by company, industry, location, and salary.

- *www.careerbuilder.com*

  A great web site for job listings and career advice.

- *www.grassisgreener.com*

  This website, Grass Is Always Greener searches over 4 million jobs

- *www.6figurejobs.com*

  This web site is designed for executives and professionals. It provides access to most of the major executive jobs, executive recruiters.

- *www.careersthroughfaith.com*

  Careers Through Faith is a wonderful website for Faith-Based Career Seminars.

- ***www.pharmaceuticaljobs-usa.com***

  This industry-specific career web site lists all positions in the Pharmaceutical & Biotechnology arena.

- ***www.financial jobs.com***

  For those individuals who are seeking opportunities in the banking, accounting, investment, or corporate finance this is one of the best web sites to peruse.

- ***www.topsalespositions.com***

  As the name implies, this web site is designed for sales professional.

- ***www.vault.com***

  This is an email-based job search service. There is lots of other nifty job search information available here as well.

- ***www.dotorgjobs.com***

  This is an excellent resource for employment opportunities in the non-profit world.

- ***www.overseasjobsexpress.com***

  This site is dedicated to those who are contemplating an overseas employment opportunity. It is a tremendous source of employment information and resources for international job-hunters.

- ***www.backdoorjobs.com***

  Backdoorjobs.com is about discovering your life's options and finding your place in the world. It shows you how to explore, dream, and discover and to turn your dreams into reality.

- ***www.snagajob.com***

  If you are looking for a part-time job, this is the website for you. It is a national database and you can apply online.

- ***www.sologig.com***

  Sologig.com is a website that is specifically designed to market your talents as an experienced freelancer, consultant, or independent professional to a nationwide audience of top employers.

- ***www.findyourspot.com***

  If you are looking to relocate you will find this resource helpful. You simply take a 10-minute quiz and they give you a free report about each "spot" they recommend, as well as a link to jobs in the area.

- ***www.salary.com***

  This website is extremely helpful to research salaries across the country in dozens of industries. It also features a job database and a salary-advice guide.

- ***www.careerjournal.com***

  This is a premier career site for executives, managers, and professionals for job searches, career advice, salary, and hiring information. It is sponsored by the Wall Street Journal.

- ***www.womensjoblist.com***

  A database dedicated to career advancement for women.

- ***www.elisabethkublerross.com***

  This is a web site that describes the life and books written by Dr. Elisabeth Kubler-Ross. Information regarding the Kuber-Ross Foundation was used with permission.

- ***www.wmbridges.com***

  This web site describes the work of Dr. William Bridges. Information regarding Dr. William Bridges Transition Model was used with permission.

- ***www.myersbriggs.org***

  This web site is the official one for the MBTI. Information used by permission of the foundation.